DATE DUE		
OCT 30		
1/17 26		
MAY 2		
FEB 18		
SEP 28		

LORDS OF THE EARTH

A HISTORY OF THE
NAVAJO INDIANS

LORDS

OF THE EARTH

BY JULES LOH

FOREWORD BY PETER MACDONALD, CHAIRMAN
THE NAVAJO TRIBAL COUNCIL

CROWELL-COLLIER PRESS, NEW YORK
COLLIER-MACMILLAN LIMITED, LONDON

TO MISS JEAN

970. 3
L

The Macmillan Company
866 Third Avenue
New York, New York 10022
Collier-Macmillan Canada Ltd., Toronto, Ontario

Printed in the United States of America

10 9 8 7 6 5 4 3 2 1

Title page photograph by Paul Conklin

FOREWORD

It is with pleasure that I have read this book which unravels the amazing story of the Navajo Nation. The tapestry of The Navajo Way is woven of many threads—ceremonialism, arts and crafts, interpersonal clan relationships, and a multiplicity of other cultural components and historical happenings—and is thus unique.

Few peoples in the history of the world have survived such vicissitudes as the author describes, and it is a matter of pride to realize that, not content with survival, The People have progressed in a manner that is the amazement of historians and others.

This narrative of the Nation's past and its present adheres closely to historical fact. It has not been necessary to embroider or over-accent any part of it. Reality speaks for itself.

As Chairman of this distinguished Tribe, I am happy to commend a book that gives such an account of its remarkable history and progress.

PETER MacDONALD
Chairman
The Navajo Tribal Council

PREFACE

This book might never have come about had not Stanley
Bartos's wormlike vehicle, guaranteed to go anywhere, become hopelessly stuck in the mossy floor of a red sandstone
canyon deep in the Navajo reservation. We were searching
the canyon for some petroglyphs Stan had come across years
before while hunting rocks. Crossing a shallow stream the
engine died and the vehicle sank inexorably in the soft sand.

What unexpected good luck! The nearest person—the
nearest dirt road—was a good twenty miles away. There
was nothing for us to do except explore the canyon leisurely
on foot and, later, camp beside the stream, have supper, and
build a warming fire of piñon knots against the chill Arizona
night.

Over the years I had spent many hours discussing with
old and young Navajos the feeling they have for their land.
But it was not until that splendid night between the upthrust
canyon walls, with only our own muted voices and the
trickle of the stream to intrude upon the quiet, that I, for a
too-brief moment, fell under the same spell the land casts
upon The People. Vast in dimension, violent in form, extrava-
gant in color, it is a land that requires time and stillness and

unhurried wandering to be comprehended. I was well aware that the only humans who truly comprehend it, who are a part of it, are the Navajos. But the awesome experience in that remote canyon at last gave me the confidence to write about The People and their land.

Thus to Stanley Bartos, and to his talented wife, LaVerne, and to their indefatigable offspring, is owed the genesis of this book—and much more. I do not profess to be either historian or anthropologist; Stan Bartos is both, and with patience, hospitality, and kindness, tutored me.

Others were also more than generous with their knowledge and research and to all of them I am most grateful: to Herbert Blatchford, a distinguished son of The People and able Indian leader, who read the manuscript and made important revisions; to Sid Moody, my colleague and friend, who pointed out its compositional flaws; to Carolyn Trager, a skillful and agreeable editor; and especially to the competent researchers and archivists at Navajo tribal headquarters in Window Rock, Arizona. I am also grateful, as they well know, to the typists who were convincing in their claim that it was fun. All together we made a book.

I have confessed that I am neither historian nor anthropologist; I should add that I am likewise neither sociologist nor missionary. There has been no shortage of any of these on the Navajo reservation over the past century nor have their efforts been in every case self-serving. Indeed, I have drawn freely upon their scholarship. My own profession is that of an observer and my relationship with The People has been on a human rather than an academic level. I believe that if the Navajos (and all American Indians) are ever to receive the full measure of justice owing them it will be because of changed attitudes at the human level.

The modest effort of this book, therefore, has been simply to introduce brother to brother in the pursuit of justice. If it helps to wash from one white mind the blind prejudice that has been the root cause of more than a century of injustice, the effort will be amply repaid.

CONTENTS

LORDS OF THE EARTH

THE PEOPLE

"WE WILL NEVER GIVE UP"

CHAPTER ONE

First Man and First Woman selected a harsh land for The People. Great, nourishing watercourses are absent, and the cloud gods do not favor the thirsty soil with much rain. The demands of living can be cruel. Yet The People complain little, for there are compensations. One, manifestly, is the exquisite beauty of the land. Across its great expanse, geologic marvels follow one after another in awesome panoply: forbidding, red rock canyons; polychrome deserts; majestic stands of ponderosa pine; gaunt, wind-carved buttes that loom against a boundless blue sky and ever change in hue and shadow and silhouette from dawn to midday to dusk.

But the main hold the land has on The People, the one unyielding attraction that reaches deep into every soul, is the profound meaning that each sculptured butte, each mesa, each golden shaft of sunshine, each soaring eagle, and each skulking coyote, holds for The People. These represent infinitely more than earthly beauty. To understand why, one must know The People.

They are the Navajo Indians. The land is theirs.

The Navajos are by far the largest remaining tribe of Indians in the United States. But that is perhaps their least distinguishing characteristic. What makes the Navajos almost unique in America's increasingly homogeneous society is their stubborn refusal to yield to the menacing melting pot. Other groups, including other Indians, seem to be blending gradually, if in some cases reluctantly, into the prevailing social landscape. Not the Navajos. The Navajos remain apart.

They remain and multiply. When Kit Carson, the redoubtable Indian-fighter and Mountain Man, led an army that laid waste The People's fields and flocks and drove them off their land a century ago, only about fifteen thousand Navajos survived. Today nearly one hundred thirty thousand live on or near their reservation. At their present birth rate, which is five times that of the United States, their number will double in a generation.

More remarkable than the Navajos' fecundity is their determination to survive as a tribe. The People want nothing so much as to preserve their culture. It is a culture so utterly different from surrounding cultures that Anglo-Americans who have lived among the Navajos for years are continually chagrined by how very little they really understand about Navajos.

All other ethnic groups in America represent subcultures. Not the Indians. The Indians are a totally distinct people. They bear no trace of Oriental, or European, or any other Old World culture. Their culture is uniquely their own, and it is complete. It served them long before a white man set foot on American soil, and it serves them well today. So distinct is the Indian culture that there is no feeling, no reaction, no interpretation that an Anglo can transfer from his culture to the Indian's with any degree of certainty. Navajos simply do not feel, do not react, and do not interpret as Anglos do. As a result the Navajo is as continually amazed at the white man as the white man is at him.

This profound fact explains why every third Navajo who strikes out from the reservation eventually returns. He discovers that the promise of a good life in the society that beckons beyond the reservation is for him often an illusion. For him the good life is the one he left, however burdened with physical hardship it might have been. His hunger might send him into the land of the Anglo, but his need to live on his own land, the territory of The People, is a stronger imperative. It draws him back.

The Navajo reservation is a 25,000-square-mile wilderness that sprawls across Arizona's northeastern quadrant and spills into New Mexico and Utah. There are few paved roads (only about 1,000 miles in a territory the size of West Virginia), though vastly more now than as recently as a decade ago. Most tourists glimpse little of Navajoland beyond the scenery along U.S. Route 66, which skirts the southern fringe, and see few Navajos other than the brooding ones who slouch against the fenders of dusty pickup trucks outside the tawdry barrooms in Gallup, New Mexico.

For some, also, the view of the Navajo's lot is influenced

by certain grim statistics of reservation life. Infant mortality, for example, is 70 percent higher on the reservation than in the nation as a whole. Life expectancy is eight years shorter. About 75 percent of Navajo men are unemployed. But those melancholy facts do not reflect the whole picture. There is truth in the biblical maxim that man does not live by bread alone.

Anyone bold enough to venture beyond the pavement to the mountains and mesas where The People live will discover a serenity unmatched anywhere. Out there, deep in the reservation, one can stand on the rim of a canyon and find no living thing within the reach of the eye except perhaps a distant hawk exploring the limitless blue sky on motionless wings; one can hear no earthly sound except an occasional sigh when the wind startles a tumbleweed. Out there, deep in the reservation, one cannot imagine a place on earth more remote, more at peace.

Or, in truth, more incongruous. A few suburban-type ranch homes can be found on the reservation, but the customary house is still the traditional hogan—a hexagonal one-room dwelling built of logs and mud with a smoke hole in the domed roof. The Navajos learned the architecture from the Ant People. Many Navajos own pickup trucks, and one even owned an airplane until free-grazing horses ate the fabric off the wings. In Navajoland, saddle horses with colorful blankets stand at hitching posts outside weathered trading posts—scenes from a railroad calendar. Inside, teenagers drink Coke from pop-top cans.

Some Navajos dress in the latest mail-order fashions, but on the reservation the ordinary attire for women and girls is the traditional Navajo fluted calico skirt that

4

brushes the ground, the bright velveteen blouse, and the richly colored blanket that drapes over their shoulders. Most Navajo men wear sturdy brogans, faded Levis, and broad-brimmed hats. But some old-timers still make fine moccasins, and some still wear their hair in a chignon, a vertical knot in back, just as their fathers and their mothers did. Both men and women display turquoise-and-silver necklaces, rings, belts, and bracelets, wearing them even while grinding corn or dipping sheep. Turquoise represents the sky—good medicine.

Many Navajos speak English, but strictly as a second language. The language of the reservation is Navajo. Few non-Navajos have mastered the language. It is incredibly difficult for Anglos to learn, not only because of its great delicacy of sound and preciseness of expression but also because it reflects so different a view of the world.

A Navajo does not say "I am hungry." He says "Hunger is hurting me." He does not say "My friend drowned." He says "Water killed my friend." From that we get a clue. Navajos regard all the world's creations, animate and inanimate, as active forces in a cosmic whole. They have little use for abstractions.

The Navajo word *tsi* means "meat," but a Navajo never uses the word in that form. By its nature, "meat" demands clarification. The meat of some unspecified creature? Then say *atsi*, "something's meat." Your own flesh? Then say *sitsi*, "my meat." Did you buy the meat at the market and want to refer to it as "my meat?" Then you must use still another prefix because you are the meat's possessor once removed. You must say *sheatsi*, literally "my something's meat." All the world's creations, animate and inanimate, are not only active forces in a cosmic whole but also are exquisitely interrelated. How one thing relates to another is important and demands precise definition.

To illustrate further, the Navajo language does not use such an expression as "he caught it." The Navajo must add prefixes and suffixes to word stems to tell what actually happened. His equivalent expression would explain whether "he" initiated the action by chasing after the thing caught or simply grabbed it as it went by. It also would specify some of the characteristics of the object caught, such as large or small, animate or inanimate, round, slender, rigid, flexible, feathered, or bald, and in what combination. "He caught it" might adequately describe to an Anglo-American the action of a baseball outfielder. Not to a Navajo. His equivalent expression would say, "He ran after and caught a small, round, rigid, inanimate object."

Language differences represent not only verbal communication obstacles but philosophical ones as well. The more thoroughly one knows another's language the better he understands that person's world view. From this superficial glance at the Navajo tongue it is evident that The People stress the concrete and insist on utmost precision in defining interpersonal relationships. Just so. To the Navajo the world is integrated and harmonious. For it to remain harmonious, an enormous number of complex relationships must be kept intact.

In the Navajo language a subtle variation in the inflection of a single syllable can completely change a word's meaning. As a result, puns provide a favorite source of Navajo humor, most of which, disappointingly, is lost in translation.

The Navajos do have a sense of humor. Some years ago the motion picture *A Distant Trumpet* was filmed on the reservation, a favorite location for making Western movies not only because of the scenery but also because of the ready supply of Indian "extras." In the film, a handsome Navajo played the part of the Indian chief who rode up to the cavalry officer to announce that he and his people had seen the light and wished to surrender. At least that was the substance of his speech as translated at the bottom of the screen. What he actually said, in flawless Navajo and admirable deadpan, was something to this effect: "White man, you are so low down you crawl on your belly like a snake. We know well your trickery and deceit. This land is ours. We will never give up." When the film was shown in Gallup, the largely Navajo theater audience was convulsed.

Very likely the Navajos won't give up, not as long as they have the sanctuary of their reservation. Down through the past century, sociologists and anthropologists have been predicting that all the old Navajo ways would vanish with the next generation—always the next. Dr. Bertha Dutton, the director of the Museum of Navajo Ceremonial Art in Santa Fe, New Mexico, mentioned a dilemma that confronts many who write about the Navajos. "I'm continually troubled over what tense to use," Dr. Dutton said. "Should I say 'the Navajos do' or 'the Navajos did'? I've found that it's always risky to assume an old custom has died out."

While it is true that each day a given number of Navajos yield to the surrounding world's unrelenting assault on their old ways, there are always replacements among the prolific tribe. Some young people exposed to Anglo influences are often all the more determined to cling to Navajo values. Chester Tso Yazzi, a talented Navajo artist, is one of them. At thirty, Chester had been abroad and had traveled in his own country from coast to coast. "The religion my children are learning," said Chester, "is the Navajo religion. I'm a Navajo."

The Navajo religion is not a rigid set of doctrines. It is more; it is the wellspring of Navajo culture. In fact, there is no word in the Navajo language for "religion." Chester Tso Yazzi used the English word merely as the closest equivalent. Navajos cannot compartmentalize their beliefs and practices as Christians seem to be able to do. Christians regard going to work and going to church as two distinct aspects of their lives. Navajos do not. To a Navajo, shearing sheep requires as much "religious" ritual as praying for rain.

A more precise word than "religion" would perhaps be "way." The Navajo Way provides The People not only with their most profound theological mysteries but also with rules for everyday social behavior. It also protects them against disease, hunger, and hardship. Indeed, it answers all their questions about every aspect of life—this life. There is no concern about an afterlife. Navajos believe that death brings neither reward nor punishment but a spiritual blending into the eternal cosmos. As one prayer in the Navajo burial rite expresses it:

> Now you go on your way alone.
> What you are now, we know not.
> To what clan you now belong, we know not.
> From now on, you are not of this earth.

The Navajo is so concerned about the precise relationships among all created things, as we have seen from his language, because he believes that everything in nature is a potential possessor of supernatural forces which he can control. If some evil occurs, sickness for example, its cause can be traced to some disruption of the world's order. The carefully ordained harmony of the cosmos has been shaken. But harmony can be restored, and the sickness thus cured, by a ritual chant. If the correct chant is sung and the ritual is performed properly, the evil will be removed. It is that simple—and that complex. The Navajo knows no prayers of supplication, nor of thanksgiving. He does not petition the supernatural; he bargains with it. The power to restore harmony rests not in any divinity but in the ceremony itself; the gods have no choice.

Each ritual is based on an age-old Navajo-myth, a story explaining how the rite began and how it must be performed. Basic among Navajo legends is the Origin Myth, which tells how First Man and First Woman led the prototypes of all creatures from the nether world, among them The People. *Navajo* is a name the Spanish gave them; to themselves they are, among the earth's creations, simply *Dineh*, The People. They do not presume that they have any greater or lesser function in the cosmic scheme than any other being or, for that matter, than the wind or the water or the sunshine.

By their legends The People know how their four sacred mountains, in the East, South, West, and North, came to be, and that all the necessities of life were deposited within their embrace. They know that Sun and his wife, Changing Woman—who manifests her awesome presence in the cycle of the seasons—gave birth to the Hero Twins, who slew all the monsters harmful to The People except four who proved useful: Hunger, Old Age, Poverty, and Dirt.

They know why the locust doesn't blink, why the gopher digs his tunnel shallow, why the hogan door must face the first light of dawn, and why one must never kill a snake, whistle in the dark, speak another's name in his presence, or laugh during a thunderstorm. They know all these things from their legends.

They learn sacred truths and gentle nursery tales, such as how the stars were placed in the sky: First Man and First Woman, resplendent in white buckskins, gathered a sackful of stars one day and began decorating the dark heavens with neat and glittering designs. When they grew tired and fell asleep, Coyote, the mischief maker, found the sack and spilled the rest of the stars helter-skelter about the sky, where they have remained in disarray to this day.

It is no doubt true that today not every Navajo knows every custom or observes every taboo. But it is safe to say that all who live on the reservation observe at least some of them, and it is easy for a blundering visitor to offend unwittingly. Once, lost on the reservation miles from any road, the author stopped at a hogan to ask directions and became friendly with the occupant, an outgoing Navajo named Guy Van Winkle. As I was leaving, Guy offered me a gift, a valuable ceremonial vase that had belonged to his late grandfather. His grandfather had been a medicine man.

"What was your grandfather's name?" I asked. Guy turned his head and mumbled a reply. "What did you say?"

Again Guy mumbled something and looked distraught.

Suddenly, utterly embarrassed, I realized that none but a gross white man who doesn't value good manners would put a Navajo in the position of having to utter a dead person's name.

The People regard a person's name as sacred, as part of his essence, and as something whose supernatural powers can erode with overuse. The name given at birth is not used in everyday life. It is spoken only on the most solemn occasions. Indeed, it is rarely known outside the immediate family. Instead, The People call one another by nicknames. Traditionally these describe a habit or a physical characteristic such as Long-Haired Boy Who Runs Fast, or Man Who Owns a Spotted Pony, names which the Navajo language can construct in a single word. But nowadays less lyrical Anglo workaday labels such as Joe Smith or Mary Jones may be assigned by a trader or a schoolteacher. Some Anglos, through ignorance or cynicism or a warped notion of cleverness, have assigned nicknames such as Pipeline, Cigarette, or Horse Trough. One old reservation document turned up a particularly intriguing name: Mona Lisa Laughing.

So numerous are the taboos governing Navajo behavior that even those who live close to The People slip at times. Stanley Bartos, a scholarly student of Navajo culture who had a home on the reservation for years, recalled a particularly embarrassing moment. A group of sheepmen had invited Stanley to dine with them. As their guest, he was offered the leg of mutton first. Without thinking, Stanley stuck the point of his knife into the meat and cut off a chunk. None of the Navajo men would eat it after that.

In Navajoland one does not stick a knife point into anything. Such a thrust resembles a lightning stroke. Anyone who eats something struck in such a way might suffer stomach pains. Slice, don't stab. In fact, don't even point. If one hands a Navajo a pencil, one should turn it sideways.

One characteristic strangers often find unsettling is that Navajos avert their eyes. They feel that looking a person directly in the eye may embarrass him, or worse, may imply that his veracity is under scrutiny. The People are much too polite for that. They are so polite that proper Navajo conduct requires no interference in any way with another's behavior, however offensive it may be. Should a Navajo want to reprove someone, he simply ignores him totally as if he did not exist. Misunderstandings between Navajos and Anglos often revolve around precisely this cultural difference. Anglos frequently misinterpret normal Navajo behavior as indifference or timidity; Navajos view accepted Anglo manners as crass rudeness.

From childhood, Navajos learn to function as members of a group, serenely tolerant of other members' foibles and failings. If a Navajo has trouble getting along off his reservation, one reason is that the white man's society pressures him to function as an aggressive individual while all his Navajo instincts demand the opposite behavior.

On the reservation, a prosperous family is expected to use its wealth for the benefit of others less fortunate, such as by holding a greater number of ceremonials. One who needs help, though, is not likely to get it unless he asks. To offer unsolicited help or advice even in such trivial matters as changing a flat tire would be considered improper interference.

No matter how "assimilated" a Navajo appears to his white brethren, if he is typical he proudly remains a

Navajo. Some often reveal their cultural differences without realizing it. There is something distinctively Navajo about the way a Navajo man wears his clothes, the way a Navajo woman uses cosmetics.

Through their history, The People have borrowed from other cultures all that could benefit them provided it fit their patterned scheme of living and rejected all else. Their traditional dress, their arts of weaving and silversmithing, parts of their mythology, and many things regarded today as uniquely Navajo actually came to them from their Pueblo Indian neighbors, from the Spanish who occupied their land for centuries, or from the conquering Americans.

The Navajos didn't exist as a tribe in the sense of an organized political unit until they were defeated and put on a reservation. The main reason there was constant trouble with The People in frontier times was that no chief spoke for all Navajos. Treaties made with one local headman were ignored by others. Even today the powers of the tribal chairman are quite limited; real authority rests in the seventy-four-member Navajo Tribal Council.

Over the years, however, the tribal concept has grown stronger rather than weaker. The more the Navajos feel their survival threatened the more intensely they cling to their common beliefs and to their land; they struggle to accommodate here and resist there the inexorable pressures of the hostile culture surrounding them. Not long ago a Navajo girl and an Anglo man decided to marry. First a Navajo ceremony was held, then a Christian ceremony. But accommodation is seldom as simple as that. For the past several years, for instance, The People have been struggling to adjust their time-honored ways of pursuing justice to American law and court procedures.

"In many fields of tribal activities where there is no controlling section or other law," said Murray Lincoln, who retired in 1970 as Navajo chief justice after sixteen years as a tribal judge, "the Navajo judges must usually submit to the guidance of tribal customs. A Navajo judge should never carry a regard for custom to a worship of them, but he must accept, as all judges should, certain traditional restraints on personal judgment. The device by which judicial action is made at all predictable on the reservation is Navajo tribal custom." Navajo judges, Mr. Lincoln continued, must analyze the facts presented to them "in the light of research not only in the law but in our tribal social and economic patterns and in light of Navajo history. And he must not rest until his opinion is convincing to the ears of his people, because in the Navajo way of life the judge's actions have little value if they are not instructive." What arbiter of justice could not benefit from such advice?

"Whenever our two cultures collide," said Mr. Lincoln, "the white man must understand that he has something to receive as well as to give." But history shows that the white man has rarely understood. Instead, almost without fail he has taken the arrogant position that his ways are better because they are his; or he has pointed to his material acquisitions as proof of cultural superiority and has righteously declared that the Navajo ought to be forced to conform for his own sake.

For the white man's sake he ought to quit trying to reshape the Navajo into his image. Because if he succeeds he will have destroyed one of the rarest and richest cultures the world has produced.

TERRA INCOGNITA

SOULS FOR THE SPANIARDS' GOD

CHAPTER TWO

Not by sailing ship from Europe but by foot from the frozen North did the first Americans arrive.

Students of man's primitive wanderings agree that the American continent was peopled by successive waves of emigrants from Siberia beginning at least thirteen thousand years ago and possibly earlier. Until about a million years ago the Asian and North American continents were connected by a vast land-bridge. Across this land-bridge walked the forefathers of the swarthy natives whom Columbus mistakenly called Indians, and the romantic cliff-dwellers of the American Southwest, whom the Navajos call *Anasazi*, The Ancient Alien Ones.

About ten thousand years ago the world suddenly grew warm. Great sheets of ice melted and the water poured back into the sea. In place of the land-bridge appeared the Bering Strait, a fifty-mile-wide waterway separating the Siberian cape from the Alaskan mainland. Emigrants who came after the great thaw could still cross the strait on winter ice; otherwise they had to come by boat.

For the boat travelers, huddled together in primitive barks, the uncharted crossing must have been a wonderful adventure. Those who experienced it surely would never forget it. One can imagine their telling and retelling the story over campfires, passing it down from father to son.

Howard Gorman, a thoughtful Navajo leader, who has great respect for his people and their traditions, has been nagged by a possibility regarding that Bering Strait crossing. The Navajo Origin Myth, he noted, includes among its most significant features an account of how the prototypes of The People had to make perilous journeys through various bodies of water before their arrival in the present world. Other parts of the legend speak of "dogs that swim in the sea." Barking seals? Gorman said he has often wondered whether these legends could have evolved from the crossing of the Bering Strait.

When the North American ice cap thawed it left a relatively warm and fertile corridor from the Alaskan coast up the Yukon River valley and down the eastern side of the Rocky Mountains. Down this path the original Americans came, tribe after tribe, representing at least eight linguistic families. Each group in its turn came southward and scattered across the inviting plains rich with grass. Some tribes turned eastward and discovered the Great Lakes, the Hudson valley, and the Florida flats. Others pushed farther, south to Mexico and South America, and developed civilizations which in full flower rivaled those of Egypt and Greece.

The Anasazi stayed in the American Southwest. In the precipitous canyon walls they built hundreds of tiny cities, all of them revealing architecture and stonework of unbelievable artistry. One, in Chaco Canyon, contained 800 rooms. Another, in Laguna Canyon, had 150 rooms. For ages, great communities inhabited these sites. They lived busy lives, laughing, loving, worshiping, and raising families. At length, probably because of a searing drought that lasted a quarter of a century, they left their cliffside homes about A.D. 1300 and pushed on to more fertile sites along the eastern flank of the Jemez Mountains.

The Anasazi were the forebears of the Pueblo tribes, who live in picturesque adobe homes still standing atop the mesas and beside the streams of the Southwest—at Acoma, Zuñi, Taos, and two dozen other mysterious, romantic places—and whose cultures greatly influenced that of the Navajo. *Pueblo* is the Spanish word for "town." The Navajo word for their Pueblo Indian neighbors is translated "Dwellers in the Earth." The Pueblo dwellings are all but indistinguishable from the cliffs and ledges on which they have nestled for generation after generation. The chronicler of Coronado's expedition described the Zuñi Pueblo as "a little crowded village looking as if it had been crumpled together."

Ask an American schoolboy the name of this country's oldest continuously inhabited city. If he's been paying attention to his textbooks, he will name Saint Augustine, Florida. The Spanish founded Saint Augustine in 1565, more than four hundred years ago. Today it is a charming tourist attraction well publicized as "the nation's oldest city." It is not. Atop bleak and barren Third Mesa in Arizona, surrounded by the Navajo reservation, is the Hopi village of Oraibi. Southeast of the Navajos, atop a towering rock island near the present-day Grants, New Mexico, is the village of Acoma. Both have been continuously occupied for at least twice as long as has Saint Augustine and probably longer. A generation before Saint Augustine's founding, Coronado counted seventy such pueblos, about thirty of which remain. Today's American Indian has nothing against Saint Augustine or its chamber-of-commerce puffs. What he does resent is a pattern of thought in America which dismisses from historical consideration much of everything that happened before the white conqueror arrived to "civilize" the land.

The Navajos were actually latecomers to the Southwest scene. They drifted down from Canada about one thousand years ago, around the time of the great Crusades in Europe. Though eons of unrecorded history obviously gave birth to their language and helped shape their culture, it is nevertheless accurate to say that their existence as a tribe, as a people, began when they took up residence in the American Southwest.

It was there among the great, red rocks and precipitous canyons that their sense of nationhood (for want of a better word) was born. The People found no need for a formal government such as developed by tribes in the East or on the Plains. Navajo social cohesion sprang from shared beliefs, a shared language, shared rules of conduct, and from one other source: the land itself. The land that The People shared was their strongest bond. This truth will become clearer later, but it is so essential to an understanding of the Navajos that it ought to be continually borne in mind. The spectacular land of the Navajos, their land, fed their bodies and fed their souls and made them a people.

Except in vague legends and obscure folk tales The People kept no record of their arrival and early residence in the Southwest, for they had no written language. Navajos know little about their earliest ancestors other than that they made their living by planting and tilling the soil, by gathering wild piñon nuts and berries, and by hunting game. (And also, be it noted, by preying mercilessly upon their Pueblo neighbors.)

The People's recorded history and the start of a new era for them began when the Spanish arrived. Having overthrown Montezuma's wealthy Aztec empire in Mexico, in 1521, the Conquistadores cast covetous eyes to the unexplored lands to the north, the *terra incognita*, as it was labeled on their crude maps. As Hernando Cortez explained to Montezuma before he put him to death, "We are troubled with a disease of the heart for which gold is the only remedy." The Spanish surmised that additional riches awaited their conquest in that unknown land. The conjecture became an obsession when they heard the wonderful tales of a remarkable adventurer, Alvar Núñez Cabeza de Vaca.

In 1528 Cabeza de Vaca found himself shipwrecked on the coast of Texas. For eight years he wandered with three companions (all of them naked, we are told) through Texas and perhaps southern New Mexico. Finally Cabeza de Vaca got to Mexico City and told fabulous stories. Eager listeners were ready to believe that the exotic people he described had just what they needed for their heart disease. Cabeza de Vaca's tales also called to mind an ancient Spanish legend. Seven Portuguese bishops, the legend goes, had fled with their flocks to a land somewhere across the western sea when the Moors conquered Spain in A.D. 734. Supposedly, the bishops founded seven cities glistening with gold and jewels—the Seven Cities of Cibola. Had Cabeza de Vaca discovered them?

The Spanish viceroy decided somebody ought to have another look. He selected for the task a trustworthy priest, Fray Marcos de Niza. Fray Marcos took with him a Moorish Negro slave named Esteban. Esteban had been one of Cabeza de Vaca's companions. Cabeza de Vaca himself had no desire for a return trip. Fray Marcos and Esteban left in the spring of 1539. By early summer the good friar was back in Mexico City with a breathtaking report. The Seven Cities of Cibola were indeed out there in that distant terra incognita! Had he seen them? Well, not actually. But he did glimpse something from a distance that looked like a city, a city larger than Mexico City. Besides, related Fray Marcos, Esteban had seen them—just before the Indians killed him. Well, Esteban hadn't exactly seen them. An Indian messenger sent by Esteban, Fray Marcos explained, had told the friar that the cities were there. Upon such events history turns.

The following summer Francisco Vásquez de Coronado set out from Mexico City leading an army and following a dream. Coronado, thirty years old, rode at the head of a column of three hundred mounted soldiers with glittering armor, flowing capes, fluttering plumes, and souls full of hope. A train of burdened mules followed the soldiers. Behind the mules trailed a flock of sheep herded by Indian and Negro slaves.

20

The fact that Coronado's main goal was an illusion does not diminish the boldness of his journey of exploration. He ventured into an unknown land, an unknown world. He was of the same breed as Columbus, Magellan, Cook, and others who followed dreams—an adventurer.

Coronado, of course, found no cities studded with turquoise and gold. He found the humble pueblos of the Zuñis and Acomas on the crags of western New Mexico and the string of pueblos along the Rio Grande, but he found no treasure. As a result the courageous Coronado upon his return to Mexico City five years later was tried for defrauding the crown. He died in humiliation in his forty-fourth year.

Coronado's empty treasure-sacks cooled Spain's ardor for a time. Exploration ceased for nearly forty years.

Then in 1582 a small expedition set out headed by Antonio de Espejo and Fray Bernardino Beltran. With a mere thirteen soldiers and a handful of slaves they probed into the very heart of Navajo country. These adventurers, too, failed to find treasure. Perhaps, looking around, they realized that what they had found was even more splendid than anything man's hand could fashion—the land itself. No cities of Cibola could match the magnificence of the ancient stone buttes of brown and yellow and red, the emerald mountains burdened with timber, the vast land sculpted by the ages—that cathedral of nature spread beneath a limitless azure dome which the Navajos called their home.

At long last the Spanish gave up their mindless search for the legendary cities and turned to a quest equally dear to their hearts. If the barbarians who dwelt in terra incognita could not produce gold for the Spaniards' treasury, at least they could provide souls for the Spaniards' God.

In 1598 another expedition journeyed northward. It was organized and led by Captain-General Juan de Oñate, reputed to be one of the five richest men in New Spain. He put up a million dollars of his own to finance the venture. Oñate's wife was the daughter of Pedro de Tovar (one of the men who had accompanied Coronado) and the great-granddaughter of Emperor Montezuma himself. Oñate's purpose was not to explore but to colonize. He aimed to stay and to become governor of the Spanish colony of New Mexico.

The expedition included 400 persons; 130 were soldiers, and the rest were families and priests. Oñate also brought along 62 oxcarts of possessions, 1,000 head of cattle, 4,000 sheep, 1,000 goats, and 300 horses. He and his indomitable pioneers established homes, built mission churches near the villages of the Pueblo Indians, and set up a town. Oñate built the town on the Rio Grande beneath the majestic Sangre de Cristo Mountains and across the river from a Pueblo named for his own patron saint, San Juan. By 1610 the area was sufficiently populated by Spaniards for them to establish a seat of government nearby at a village they had begun building the previous year. They had named the village La Villa Real de la Santa Fé de San Francisco. It soon came to be known simply as Santa Fe, Holy Faith.

Thus the Spaniards, unbidden, came to the land of The People—and remained. In 1670, without consulting or informing the residents who had been there more than seven hundred years before them, the Spaniards declared that the land belonged to them.

INDIOS BARBAROS

"RAISED LIKE THE DEER"

CHAPTER THREE

In their *entradas* northward the Spanish, not surprisingly, paid considerably more attention to the Pueblo Indians than to the Navajos. The Conquistadores were looking for cities of gold. Humble pueblos were a far cry from that, but they at least fit the broad definition of cities. Moreover, the Pueblo Indians were stationary. They could be counted on to be in the same place when the next explorer came along following his rude map.

To the Spanish, the Navajos were *indios bárbaros*, "wild men." They were not urbanized like proper Europeans. In a more scholarly vein, the Spanish at first called The People *Apaches de Navajo*. The first word, *Apache*, referred to the linguistic group to which a number of Southwest tribes belonged. It is somewhat remarkable that the Spanish recognized this common linguistic trait at that early date.

The larger linguistic family, of which the Apacheans were a branch, were the Athapascans. Various other Athapascan tribes who made the Bering Strait crossing stopped off in interior Alaska, western Canada, and on the northwestern Pacific coast of the United States.

The Apachean members pushed on to the American Southwest. Other Apachean tribes included the Lipans, Kiowas, Chiricahuas, Mescaleros, and Jicarillas. The Pueblo Indians, who arrived much earlier, were of an entirely different linguistic family which broke down into related dialects of its own.

At the time of Columbus and Coronado, whose journeys of exploration were only a half century apart, about 550 Indian languages were spoken in North America. Many Indians were bilingual, but for the most part they used a universal sign language which they developed to communicate with one another. None had developed a written alphabet, although the Cherokee scholar Sequoyah would much later.

Linguistic differences began to appear among the various Apachean tribes about the time of Coronado. Their languages would always remain more or less related, and related as well to the tongues of their Athapascan cousins who stayed in the Canadian North. One studious Navajo reported that he had heard about Navajo soldiers serving in World War II who were able to understand various dialects they encountered in parts of Asia. Linguists tend to doubt the story. It seems just as farfetched as the report of an American soldier who guarded the Navajos during their captivity in the 1860s: "Persons who speak the

Welsh language find no difficulty in understanding them." Some Welsh-speaking soldier apparently played a nice joke on his comrades.

How the Spanish arrived at their original term for The People—*Navajo*—is not at all certain. In Spanish the word could mean either a type of clasp knife or a flat, worthless piece of land. Or it might have been the Spanish corruption of a word meaning "cultivated fields" in the Tewa language (spoken by some of the Pueblo Indians). The seventeenth-century Spanish friar, Alonzo de Benavides, referred to the Navajos as "the Apaches of the great planted fields." Perhaps *Navajo* combines both derivations. In any event, after a few decades they came to be known as Navajos to the Spanish and to all who followed. To themselves they remained simply *Dineh*, The People.

Wild men they may have been to early Spanish explorers, but there is no record of the Navajos regarding those first invaders with similar derogation. The opposite was true. Up until the Spaniards began shooting at them, both the Pueblo Indians and the Navajos had welcomed the Spaniards.

The People were continually borrowing from other cultures to enrich their own. They regarded the Pueblo Indians, for example, with awe. Navajo chants and legends acknowledge the Pueblo Indians' many cultural accomplishments and especially the power of their religious ceremonies. So The People absorbed portions of the Pueblo ceremonials into their own rites, altering them with a subtle genius that made the borrowed trait characteristically Navajo. The Navajo culture is an amalgamation of other cultures, yet it is totally Navajo. Somehow all traces of the original owners have vanished. The process might be called "creative imitation." It is a uniquely Navajo talent and probably the most important characteristic of the tribe, because the trait has assured the tribe's survival no matter how jarring its collisions with other cultures may be.

The Conquistadores rode into Navajoland on horses. The friars who accompanied them brought along flocks of sheep. The Navajo marvelled at both animals; he had never seen either. Before long, sheep and horses revolutionized Navajo life.

Originally hunters and farmers, The People had become by the early seventeenth century, a hundred years after the first Spaniards arrived, a well-established, pastoral society. Their flocks soon numbered tens of thousands; hunger was no longer a constant threat. As their horse herds multiplied, their hunting and raiding prowess expanded. Sheep and horses came to be referred to by The People as "that which men live by," items critical to their culture. Horses, especially, became symbols of personal wealth and dignity and remain so today.

For year after year, century after century, the fair-skinned Spaniards trekked in ever increasing numbers to the ancient land that for a millennium The People had considered theirs. Adventurous military *adelantados* followed the trails mapped by Coronado, and after them came more pioneers to the settlements of Oñate and to private land grants issued to them by the King of Spain. And horses and sheep were not all they brought with them. They also brought strange medicine men, Long Coats, who tried to convince The People of a strange God.

In that endeavor one can only admire the persistence of

the friars. From the beginning the priests never had much luck with conversions. Indeed, in 1675 the Spanish governor decided to lend a hand by suppressing all "superstitious practices." If persuasion wouldn't work, force might. To show he meant it, his soldiers hanged three Pueblo medicine men and jailed forty-four others.

The Pueblo Indians smouldered. Five years later one of the medicine men who had been jailed, a determined man named Popé, consulted with the elders of the Taos Pueblo and hatched a plot. It would require the cooperation of every pueblo as well as the alliance of the Apaches and the Navajos—a degree of cooperation the Indians of the territory had never before achieved and never would again. Somehow Popé arranged it.

On a prearranged date, August 10, 1680, every pueblo rose up as one, and the outraged warriors slaughtered every Spaniard in reach, about a fifth of the total population of twenty-five hundred. They destroyed the Spaniards' homes and possessions and stacked the bodies of their priests on the hated altars of the churches. Then they chased the terrified survivors all the way down the Rio Grande to the Mexican border. The Spanish dared not venture northward for another twelve years, and it actually was sixteen years before they were able to reconquer the Pueblo Indians in the name of God and the King of Spain.

They began their missionary efforts anew with awesome persistence. Eventually the priests could claim a measure of success in converting the Pueblo Indians. They did not convert them, actually, for the Pueblo Indians seemed to accept Christianity as a supplement to their own beliefs, not a replacement.

With the Navajos they had practically no success at all. The priests did manage to win over, at least to the extent that the Pueblo Indians were won over, a few, small groups in scattered areas around Cebolleta on the eastern fringe of Navajoland. To this day the Navajos refer to these groups as *Dineanaih,* The People Who Are Enemies. Years later, Indians from these groups acted as scouts for the white soldiers bent on exterminating The People. The great majority of the Navajos were far less responsive to the Long Coats' invitations. One friar reported that a Navajo told him The People "could not become Christians because they had been raised like the deer." They chose to remain like the deer, free to live in their own, natural way.

Occasionally Navajo parents would, in exchange for gifts, allow the friars to sprinkle their children with water. It seemed to please the *padres* and do no harm to the children. Apparently those *indios bárbaros* all looked alike to the friars because there is evidence that the same parents, in exchange for more gifts, brought their children around to be baptized again and again. One Spanish document reported no fewer than sixty thousand conversions —about three times the total estimated Indian population of the entire territory at the time.

When the Spaniards embarked on their reconquest of the Pueblo Indians after their twelve-year exile, many Pueblo families fled their villages and went to live among the Navajos. It was during this period that The People developed their famous talent for spinning and weaving wool. They learned the art from the Pueblo Indians. As with other cultural acquisitions, their weaving became distinctively Navajo. Indeed it became the talent for which they were to become most famous. Navajos are able to assimilate thoroughly the arts of others; for example, they even developed over the centuries a legend which tells in fascinating detail how in antiquity Spider Woman—a mythological figure who dwells atop an eight-hundred-foot pinnacle in Canyon de Chelly—taught The People the art of weaving. For that reason Navajo women were the weavers; among the Pueblo Indians only the men wove. So swiftly did The People raise weaving to a high art that one Spanish governor could only marvel. "They work their wool with more delicacy and taste than the Spaniards," he reported.

Most of the Navajos' contacts with the Spanish were neither to barter blankets nor to have their children sprinkled but to raid the fleecy flocks of the settlements. Most of the "wars" referred to in old Spanish documents were in fact either forays by the Navajos or punitive expeditions by the Spanish. The Spanish also felt that their Christian duty was to steal as many Navajo children as they could, chain them to pews for catechism instructions, and then allow them to become slaves after they had proven their docility. One friar described the Navajos as "wayward if lovable children, to be kept in permanent bondage." Such treatment was granted official sanction by the king in the *Reglamento de 1772*, the Indian policy for the province. The Navajos retaliated in a way that might be expected—by stealing Spanish children. There was one difference. A Spanish child thus stolen became a full-fledged member of the Navajo family into which he was adopted. The People had no provision in their social system for second-class citizenship or racial discrimination.

To punish the Navajos the Spanish frequently enlisted the aid of Pueblo warriors. For example, when a small Navajo band raided the pueblo of Jemez and killed the chief, the Spanish provincial-governor mounted a *junta de guerra*, a "war party," against The People with a force composed of 50 soldiers and 212 Pueblo auxiliaries. Their retaliation was brutal. The army killed 30 Navajos; captured 7; and took 316 bushels of corn, 11 head of cattle, and 110 sheep.

It rarely mattered to the governor whether the Navajos his soldiers found and punished were the guilty ones or not. On one occasion a group of innocent Ute Indians were rounded up along with some Navajos and brought to Santa Fe for punishment. When a party of Ute chieftains came to protest, the governor had them slain on the spot, in the audience chamber of the palace. After that Utes, too, swept down on white settlements to pillage and burn.

One especially memorable retaliatory raid took Spanish soldiers into the very heart of the Navajo stronghold and resulted in one of the most hideous massacres in history.

The Navajo stronghold was Canyon de Chelly. (Its name was derived from a Spanish effort to pronounce the Navajo word *tsegi,* which means "canyon." It comes out sounding like shay-y; the Spanish language doesn't have an adequate reproduction of the Navajo's glottal *g.*) The canyon is a Y-shaped crevice with sheer rock walls rising as high as a thousand feet from its moist, fertile floor. Its precipitous walls contain numerous niches and over-hangs. Crouched within and beneath them, The People could feel safe from any enemy attacking from above. Or should an attack come from below, the enemy marching up the canyon floor would be vulnerable to Navajo arrows and rocks hurled from the heights. Canyon de Chelly was a fortress of utmost security.

Thus it was straight to Canyon de Chelly that a group of Navajos fled one day in 1805 when they were being pursued by a troop of Spanish soldiers with guns. The Navajo women and children took refuge in a large cave high on the wall of one arm of the canyon. The Navajo men pushed noisily on, hoping to lure the pursuing Spaniards past the hiding women and children.

The ruse didn't work. The soldiers spied the women and children in the cave above them. Riflemen clambered as high as they could up the rocks on the opposite side of the canyon from the Navajos' lofty refuge and from there fired at the sloping roof of the rock cave. They fired and reloaded, fired and reloaded, fired, and fired again. The murderous musket-balls ricocheted like summer hail upon the women and children and riddled their cowering bodies.

Meanwhile, other soldiers had discovered the perilous hand-and-toe trail leading to the cave. They climbed it and entered the cave. In an orgy of bloodletting they thrust bayonets through every person in the cave down to the last hysterical mother and wailing baby. Then they methodically crushed the skulls of the dead and dying women and children with their gun butts. During the horror some of the Navajo women, insane with terror, dropped their babies from the cliff in the futile hope that a miracle might snatch them from certain death by Spanish bayonets.

Not a person survived. From that day the cave became known as Massacre Cave and that arm of the canyon as *El Cañon del Muerto*, The Canyon of the Dead. The People did not want to forget the Spanish and what they had wrought. On the cliff face of El Cañon del Muerto is a Navajo painting of a Spanish military unit accompanied by a priest.

If there was a change in official policy toward the *indios bárbaros* when Mexico declared its independence from Spain in 1821, it was not discernible to the Navajos. The only difference they could notice was that the settlements of the invaders grew more rapidly. Wealthy cattle-barons and miners arrived to build their fortunes in the new nation. Ragged mestizos and Indian and Negro hirelings followed, as well as the inevitable bands of drifters, fugitives, and rogues.

To the Mexican as to the Spaniard before him, the status of the Navajo in the territory was clear. His fleecy flocks and fawn-eyed women were fair game.

THE NEW MEN

CHAPTER FOUR

The East, the home of Dawn Boy and Father Sun, was the direction in Navajo mythology whence all blessings flowed. What irony. Of all the horrors visited upon The People during three centuries of Spanish and Mexican occupation of their homeland, none equalled the fate that was to befall them at the hands of a new assemblage of Europeans rapidly gathering on the shores of the great ocean which The People vaguely knew existed far beyond the eastern horizon. They were the Americans. At their hands in mid-nineteenth century the Navajos were destined to undergo one of the most wrenching ordeals any people have ever endured. The Navajos would refer to it as "The Long Walk" and would reckon all dates from that climactic episode.

Practically from the day the *Mayflower* landed the Americans expressed clearly the attitude they would maintain toward the inhabitants of the land to which they had fled seeking liberty. Cotton Mather, the celebrated Congregationalist minister, wrote, after his colonial Christian flock had slaughtered six hundred Pequot Indians, "The woods were almost cleared of those pernicious creatures, to make room for a better growth."

A century and a half later, on November 3, 1755, the governing council at Boston issued a proclamation. In this instance it concerned the Penobscot tribe and read in part: ". . . I do hereby require his Majesty's subjects of the Province to embrace all opportunities of pursuing, captivating, killing and destroying all and every of the aforesaid Indians." To make genocide more attractive to His Majesty's subjects, the proclamation continued:

> *For every scalp of a male Indian brought in as evidence of their being killed as aforesaid, forty pounds. For every scalp of such female Indian or male Indian under the age of twelve years that shall be brought in as evidence of their being killed as aforesaid, twenty pounds.*

The English, however, could not claim credit for introducing the quaint practice of scalping to the American continent. That distinction belonged to the Dutch. They were paying for Indian scalps as early as 1641, and the policy effectively cleared southern New York and New Jersey of "pernicious creatures." By the middle of the eighteenth century a male Indian scalp was going for the equivalent of $134 and a female scalp for $50 in the Quaker colony of Pennsylvania.

Killing Indians, especially mature male ones, became a

more profitable pursuit in the budding American nation than trapping beavers, and it involved about the same moral scruples. In the West, at about the same period, the Spanish used another method of counting Indian bounties. They cut off the ears of their victims—equally effective but requiring more bookkeeping.

Some found it troublesome to shoot or club Indians to death and looked for more efficient ways. During the French and Indian War in 1763 Lord Jeffrey Amherst, the British colonial-commander, distributed among the Indians blankets infected with smallpox from the hospital at Fort Pitt.

Like the Spaniards across the continent, the colonials in the East were quick to realize that one good way to rid the woods of Indians was to bring them to the city—in chains. The Massachusetts Bay colonists captured all the Indian slaves they could, selling the ones they didn't need to their fellow Puritans in Bermuda. Farther south, in North Carolina, Col. James Moore reported in 1704, "I . . . have killed and taken as slaves 325 men, and have taken as slaves 4,000 women and children." He was talking about Indians. Four years later South Carolina reported among its population 1,100 adult Indian slaves.

America has romanticized in storybooks and rhymes its picturesque Indian heroes from Powhatan to Tecumseh, Massasoit to Hiawatha, and King Philip to Chief Joseph. America has manifested attachment to its Indian heritage in countless lyrical place-names such as Chattanooga, Omaha, Delaware, Minnesota, Susquehanna, and Mississippi; indeed, twenty states have Indian names. America has professed only the most laudatory humanitarianism from the beginning, when the United States Congress on

August 7, 1789, enacted the provisions of the Northwest Territory Ordinance, which declared: "The utmost good faith shall always be observed towards the Indians, their lands and property shall never be taken from them without their consent; and in their property, rights and liberty, they shall never be invaded or disturbed. . . ." America has made 389 treaties with Indians, usually guaranteeing them sanctuary "as long as waters run and the grass shall grow" or in other language similarly condescending to the Indians' supposedly primitive level of understanding.

Despite all of that, the bitter truth remains. The United States of America, in the century and a half before it became a republic and for more than a century thereafter, pursued with zeal and efficiency only one consistent policy toward the native inhabitants of the American soil—the policy of extermination.

The problem with the Indians was that they didn't "use" the land properly. White people, on the other hand, used the land "according to the intentions of the Creator," said Thomas Hart Benton, the first senator from Missouri. There was only one solution. The Indians had to be gotten rid of to make way for a people with a better understanding of the Creator's intentions. Congress gave the process official sanction in the Indian Removal Act of 1830.

By that decree thousands were herded, with whatever meager possessions they could carry, along various "trails of tears" to the supposedly worthless prairies west of the Mississippi. Some even got there. When it was discovered that the prairies weren't worthless after all but were extremely fertile croplands, the Indians, of course, had to be uprooted once again. Never mind the government's pledge that the lands were to be theirs forever. They were sent next to an arid waste benevolently set aside as "permanent" Indian Territory and solemnly assured that they would never be disturbed again. Alas, the Creator's intentions were otherwise. Not many years later this land became the Oklahoma Territory, and most of it was opened up to whichever white settlers could get there first.

After the American Civil War, Gen. William Tecumseh Sherman, who, notwithstanding his middle name, believed that "treachery is inherent in the Indian character," was put in charge of protecting the emigrants to the plains. Some of the Indians, resentful of being robbed of their land, treacherously attempted to fight back. "The more we can kill this year the less will have to be killed the next war," Sherman wrote in 1868 to his brother John, a United States senator, "for the more I see of these Indians the more convinced I am that all have to be killed or maintained as a species of pauper. Their attempts at civilization are simply ridiculous."

Sherman received full support for this view from his superior, Gen. Ulysses S. Grant. A month before Grant was elected president he agreed publicly that white emigrants must be protected "even if the extermination of every Indian tribe was necessary to secure such a result." On July 7, 1876, almost a century to the day after the signing of the Declaration of Independence, *The New York Times* reported that "high officers" in the War Department advocated "the policy of extermination of the Indians and think the speedier the better its accomplishment." These officers, the paper concluded, regarded the Indian wars as "wars of annihilation."

As early as April 21, 1836, the Indians east of the Mississippi had been fairly well wiped out. Or rather, in the euphemism of the time, they had been removed. That was the day when a small army of volunteers shouting the battle cry, "Remember the Alamo!" smashed a well-organized Mexican force twice its size along the San Jacinto River near Galveston, Texas. The United States promptly recognized Texas an an independent republic and, much to the irritation of Mexico, listened sympathetically to Texas's request to become a state. Annexation came in 1846 when the visionary James K. Polk took office as president.

By then America was astir with the idea of westward expansion. John C. Frémont of the United States Army's topographical corps had explored the land all the way to California. Frémont was not the first to explore the West. Fur trappers and adventure-loving individualists, the Mountain Men as they were called, had blazed trails before him. But Frémont had the advantage of being married to a senator's daughter and having the famed Kit Carson, a Mountain Man himself, as a guide and scout. Frémont's accounts of his journeys were widely circulated in the press.

At about the same time another article in the public press further excited America's adventurous spirit. An editorial in the *New York Morning News* in December, 1845, talked of "our manifest destiny to overspread and to possess the whole of the continent which Providence has given us for the development of the great experiment of liberty and federated self-government."

"Manifest destiny"—the words had a prophetic ring. Before long they were a part of the political vocabulary of many Americans.

The trouble was, a huge chunk of Mexico extended well

up into the continent which the New York editorial writer considered to be Providence's gift to America. Indeed, Mexico possessed all of the land which constitutes the present states of Arizona, New Mexico, Utah, Nevada, and California, and parts of Wyoming and Colorado. Mexico's possession of all this land, like Spain's possession of it earlier, was of course never recognized by the people who had lived upon it from its first settlement.

To the whites who beheld that vast domain, the prize of the lot was California. England and France had covetous eyes on California, but so did America, and President Polk was determined that neither European power would get its hands on it. Polk offered to buy California from Mexico, but Mexico wouldn't sell. He also offered to buy New Mexico for $5 million—no deal.

Not only was Mexico adamant, but Mexicans were still chafing over the annexation of Texas as the twenty-eighth American state. In Mexico City, anti-American feelings were at the boiling point; in Washington, war hawks clamored to teach Mexico a lesson. All that was needed was an incident to light the fuse.

On April 25, 1846, an American patrol under Gen. Zachary Taylor—while prowling a piece of territory north of the Rio Grande which was claimed by both the United States and Mexico—ambushed a Mexican patrol. Eleven Americans were killed. General Taylor fired off a message to Washington saying, "hostilities may now be considered as commenced." On May 13, America declared war. A few in Congress were ashamed and appalled. Congressman Lincoln of Illinois declared to the House that the war had been "unnecessarily and unconstitutionally commenced."

It was war nonetheless, and for four months it raged

south of the Rio Grande. Meanwhile, another American force was in the field. It saw no combat, but its importance in the eventual conquest was not diminished by that fortuitous situation. It was the United States Army of the West, and its mission was to take possession of the Mexican territories north of the Rio Grande from Santa Fe to the Pacific coast.

The commander of the Army of the West was Brig. Gen. Stephen Watts Kearny, a trim, fifty-two-year-old professional soldier with pale eyes, seamed cheeks, and gray hair brushed forward on his brow. He possessed gallant charm and a dashing appearance in his long, blue coat piped in gold with gold epaulets and twelve gold buttons. He was candid but not brusque. All who knew him regarded him as a gentleman of his word.

On a sultry morning in August, General Kearny and his 1,658 men arrived in the sun-parched village of Las Vegas, New Mexico. He had expected armed resistance from the Mexicans, but there was none. Without hindrance, Kearny rode into the town plaza, summoned the citizens, and mounted a rooftop to address them.

He told them who he was, and who the men with him were—soldiers of the United States of America. The men did not look very soldierly. They wore no uniforms. Their beards were ragged; their hair, long and uncombed. All except 300 of them were volunteers—soldiers of fortune —and from the easy way they held their muzzle-loaders and wore their knives they gave the impression that they could hold their own in a fight. General Kearny, on the other hand, was awesome in his soldierly bearing.

He had come, he told the villagers, to inform the people of the New Mexico Territory that they should regard themselves thereafter as citizens of the United States of America. He said that they need not fear his conquest, for "not a pepper, not an onion, shall be disturbed or taken." He gave them added assurance: "The Navajos come down from the mountains and carry off your sheep and your women whenever they please. My government will correct all this. They will keep off the Indians, protect you in your persons and property."

The general remounted and rode at the head of his men to Santa Fe. Again, he met no resistance. At Santa Fe, on August 15, General Kearny read another proclamation, this one from the roof of the Palace of the Governors. When he finished, one of his troopers hauled down the red, white, and green flag of Mexico and ran up a banner of red, white, and blue. Then the general set out for California. With him, as guide, went a man who knew the Southwest as few others—Kit Carson.

The Navajos called the Americans the "New Men." With their arrival, one era ended for The People and a new one began.

One could forgive the Navajos a collective sigh of despair at General Kearny's pronouncement. He had referred to the conquered New Mexicans as new citizens of the United States; what was to be the Navajos' status? As for his reference to raiding, surely the New Men must have known that the road of plunder had been traveled both ways. True, Navajo raids on the Spaniards' livestock once became so effective that the settlers had to send to Spain for a new supply of horses; but that was back in 1775. Since then, especially since Mexico's independence, it was equally true that The People were more sinned against than sinning.

"I think the Navajos have been the most abused people on the continent," Dr. Louis Kennon, who had lived in the territory for years, told a senate investigating committee. In all hostilities the Mexicans have always taken the initiative with but one exception that I know of. When I first came here the Navajos were at peace, and had been for a long time. There was a pressure brought to bear—to make war on the Navajo—and if you asked the Mexicans any reason for making war, they would give no reason but that the Navajo had a great many sheep and horses and a great many children."

Sheep, horses, and children—to the Mexican raider they had equal status and were all fair game. Human slavery was a custom in which the invaders, including the New Men, were far more accomplished than the *indios bárbaros*.

Dr. Kennon had a chance to observe the practice at first hand. "I think the number of captive Navajo Indians held as slaves to be . . . from five to six thousand," he testified. "I know of no family which can raise one hundred and fifty dollars but what purchases a Navajo slave, and many families own four or five, the trade in them being as regular as the trade in pigs or sheep."

In view of all of that, General Kearny's promise to protect the settlers from the Indians must have sounded to Navajo ears like a promise to protect the coyotes from the lambs.

But that could not have been the general's only remark that bemused The People. General Kearny had claimed literal possession of the land for the New Men, just as the Mexicans and the Spaniards had claimed it in their turns. But the land was not theirs, it belonged to none of them. It was the land of The People, and The People had yielded it to no man. To a Navajo, no lordly proclamation however imposingly read from a rooftop could change that. The People could be driven off, sold like cattle, and decimated, but the land would still be theirs. It was theirs from the beginning, from their beginning as a people, and would remain so until their end.

DINETAH

CHAPTER FIVE

The Navajos' claim to a particular piece of geography in the American Southwest did not rest merely on the basis of prior settlement, though that should have been sufficient. They were not the first people to live there, but they were the first to stay, with the exception of the Pueblo tribes, whose territory they never claimed. The People recognized the right of the Pueblo Indians to their ancient villages, which dotted the landscape. Though the Navajos raided the villages time and again, it was never with the intent of driving the Pueblo Indians away or of taking their land. The Navajos drove no one away. They lusted after no additional territory. They desired not one square inch more than what they had considered rightfully theirs from their beginning.

Nor was their claim to the land based on some private covenant with a god, such as moved the children of Abraham to claim the land of Canaan, though that analogy comes closer. The Navajos' claim to their land was deeper, and different.

The Navajo knew the land was his not because of any legalistic reasoning but because every fiber of his being told him so. He was born to the land and was a part of the land, as much a part of it as its red canyons and purple buttes. And the land was part of him. He could never be entirely separated from his land.

The People came up from beneath the earth, from the Fourth World to the Fifth—or present—World at a point near Hesperus Peak in the La Plata mountain range of southwestern Colorado. In the Navajo tongue the place is called Where We Emerged.

Before their emergence, life in the Fourth World was for eons most serene. That world was a land surrounding a great, axial rock, the Mountain Around Which Moving Was Done. This great mountain was also surrounded by four sacred mountains, in the East, South, West, and North. The Fourth World was The People's Eden.

It was not a serpent that spoiled this happy life; it was Coyote, the Navajos' eternal troublemaker. One day Coyote, with a sunbeam lasso, caught a tiny water monster and pulled him out of the holy river that flowed through the land. The monster was the infant son of the god named Grabs Things in Deep Water.

Suddenly a chill swept over the land. All the creatures of the air flocked together in a great swarm, terrified. A cold wind rushed in from the North, the South, and the West. A flood began to rise.

First Man and First Woman, the prototypes of The People, took action. They gathered all the seeds of plants, dirt from the four sacred mountains of East, South, West, and North; and all other things necessary for existence. Then they led all the creatures and The People to the top of the great rock in the center of their land, the Mountain Around Which Moving Was Done, to escape the flood.

The swirling waters chewed at the hill and turned it into a mass of mud. First Man and First Woman immediately planted a tree, a fir tree, and ordered the creatures to climb it. It did not grow tall enough. The situation was desperate.

Miraculously, two beings appeared. "Help us!" someone cried out to them. The two approached. Then one of them turned deliberately and left the group, retreating beyond earshot. "Who is that?" they asked the second being. Making sure his companion was beyond hearing range, he replied, "He is my maternal uncle. He is the Sun."

The Sun returned to the group, and the second being, in like fashion, withdrew until he was out of earshot. "Who is that?" they asked the Sun; and the Sun replied, "He is my maternal uncle. He is the Moon."

The People did not question the mysterious relationship, and they learned from that incident never to speak another's name in his presence. They have kept the rule faithfully.

The water rose incessantly. At length the Sun stuck a long, reed flute into the mud of the dissolving mountain. The Moon did likewise with a pine-tree flute. The two flutes soared high into the heavens, twin arks, as it were, to save all living things from the deluge.

The creatures and The People scrambled into the flutes

and climbed up, up toward the Fifth World. Last to enter was Turkey, who made it just in time. Indeed, the foaming tide was lapping at the base of the flute as he entered, and the foam bleached the tip of his tail permanently white.

First to emerge in the Fifth World was Locust. He peered out with utmost caution, daring not to let down his guard in that critical moment of uncertainty. "Don't even blink! Don't even blink!" said the Child of the Wind to Locust, whispered the Child of the Wind into Locust's ear. Locust did not blink, and has not blinked since. And The People learned that it would be foolish indeed ever to disregard the whispered warnings of the Child of the Wind.

Alas, there was disappointment—the Fifth World was entirely water. And floating leisurely upon the water were four monsters: one in the South, a blue one; one in the West, yellow; one in the North, black; and one in the East, white. Each monster carried a glistening weapon, a knife of the finest obsidian.

The black monster rushed at Locust and made a pass with his knife. The other three in turn did the same. And that is why the masked dancers, the *Yei*, rush menacingly from the four directions at Navajo children in their initiation ceremony, so that the children will learn never to shut their eyes in fear and thus perchance go blind.

Locust pleaded with the monsters. "Make the water go away," he urged. "We are threatened with water from below as well." The monsters refused.

"All right," said Locust, "I will make a proposition. If you can repeat a trick that I can do, we will return below. If not, you must let us come up." The monsters accepted the challenge. Locust took two feathered objects. He stroked them across his mouth then passed them through a passage in his chest, pushing one through from one side and one from the other. Crossing his arms, he drew them out from opposite directions. The water monsters were not able to do the trick. They did not have a chest like Locust's. They agreed to let The People and the creatures emerge.

But how could they? It was a world of water. Locust summoned Mountain Sheep. With his huge horn, Mountain Sheep dug a deep gorge for the water to flow out. The gorge, called the Grand Canyon, is still there on the western rim of Navajoland. The instrument that dug it, the sheep's horn, is still there too, rising majestically from the canyon floor. Since that day The People have venerated mountain sheep horn as a sacred substance.

The exodus from the Fourth World had begun, but the pace was slow. The hole was too narrow, and the water from below was rising inexorably. Badger was summoned and told to make the hole larger. He did, burrowing furiously upon his belly. As a result, Badger's belly became stained black, to remain so forever.

At length the long procession from the nether world was over. In all the excitement, however, an important matter was overlooked. Concealed in his armpit, Coyote still had the infant son of the Fourth World water monster that he had caught with a sunbeam. The People urged Coyote to put him back. Coyote said no, whereupon the infant monster's father turned his son into thunder and lightning, evermore to terrify The People when water rains down from above.

As the flood of the Fifth World poured out through the

sheep-horn gorge, the earth was being left a soggy morass. First Man and First Woman summoned the Wind. The Wind blew four days, but the earth remained soft. Fox Squirrel planted grass, foxtail grass. Other creatures planted trees. The plants held. Their roots drank up the moisture, and the earth hardened.

Now it was time for First Man and First Woman to set the sacred mountains in place, the four mountains they had brought from the world below.

They placed the first one in the East, the direction of the rising Sun. They fastened the mountain down with a lightning bolt and adorned it with White Shell and White Corn. They placed Male Rain upon it—hard, driving rain. They named the mountain *Sisnajini*. The white man gave it another name, Mount Blanco. It is in the Sangre de Cristo range in Colorado.

The next mountain they placed in the South. They fastened it down with a knife of blue flint, decorated it with a blue feather, Turquoise, and Yellow Corn. They placed upon it sweet, gentle rain—Female Rain—and named the mountain *Tsodzil*. The white man named it Mount Taylor. It is in the San Mateo range near the city of Grants.

The third mountain they put in the West. They fastened it with a sunbeam, decorated it with Abalone, and named it *Dokaoslid*. It is the twin-peaked mountain the white man calls San Francisco Peaks, near Flagstaff, Arizona.

The fourth mountain they set near the place of their emergence, in the North. They fastened it with a rainbow and adorned it with Jet and a black feather, and named it *Dibentsa*. It is known as Hesperus Peak to the white man.

Within the divine protective embrace of the four sacred

mountains lies *Dinetah*, The Land of The People—their land.

Those are the boundaries. Within them life is possible and happiness assured, provided that one lives in accord with the rules set down by the Holy Ones and remains in harmony with the world about him. Beyond those boundaries life is uncertain, happiness impossible. The Holy Ones who dwell in the four mountains provided mountain prayers and mountain songs for The People, the rituals by which they can always restore harmony when things go wrong. Within the mountains' heights are the perfect models of everything necessary to man's well-being—the perfect ear of corn, the perfect sheep, the perfect singer, and the perfect song—the prototypes, the sources of renewed life for man's imperfect copies of these essentials in the land the mountains smile down upon. To the Navajos the land within the sacred mountains is where the world of The People blends with the world of the gods. To the Navajos, Dinetah thus represents the closest approximation man can hope to find of heaven on earth. Beyond the boundaries of the sacred mountains, prayers and songs lose their meaning and ceremonials become merely nostalgic folk rituals.

The Holy Ones placed other sacred landmarks in Dinetah, each steeped in mythological adventure.

The People can look northward to Black Rock and know it as the place where First Man taught them one of the sand paintings used in the Blessing Way ceremony. On Sierra Blanca Peak another sand painting was given, on Gobernador Knob a healing ritual. Atop Chuska Mountain, Beautiful Mountain, and Agathla Peak just south of Monument Valley, the Sky Supporters stand holding aloft Dinetah's sweeping canopy of blue. In the Northwest rises Navajo Mountain in the shape of a great bird with a red, rock comb—a holy place. In the Northeast, visible for a hundred miles, is twin-spired Shiprock (as the Anglos call it), which The People know as Winged Rock—the petrified remains of the eagle-like Rock Monster of sacred legend. In the Southeast is the lava flow near Grants—the dried blood of a monster slain by Child of the Water and Monster Slayer, the Hero Twins.

No, the Navajos need no precise survey, no legal deed, no carefully drawn lines of latitude and longitude to know the land that is theirs. They know it in their souls. Long before history took note of them, the Navajos and their gods had woven a lasting mythological web among their four sacred mountains, and it has held them together as a people. For them it envelops every living and nonliving thing therein. It gives sacred meaning to every feather, every stripe, and every petal; to the Wind and the Rain and the Sunbeam; to the Coyote and the Locust and the Squirrel; and to the mesa and the mountain and the meadow. The Land of The People, Dinetah, is their destiny—their manifest destiny.

THE GOLDEN AGE

LORDS OF THE EARTH

CHAPTER SIX

There in the sanctuary of their sacred mountains, there among the spectacular shrines their Holy Ones had provided on every horizon, there upon a benevolent Mother Earth and beneath a gracious Father Sun, The People lived and prospered.

Navajo prosperity seemed to grow with the development of Navajo mythology; it is not certain which nurtured which. The People contend that health of mind and spirit inevitably brings physical well-being rather than the other way around. From the time of the Pueblo Indian revolt of 1680 until the arrival of the New Men in 1846, The People expanded their sheep flocks; brought new beauty and industry to their weaving; added charm to their dress; planted an increasing number of acres in corn, a holy crop; tended fruit orchards and melon fields in the lush canyon bottoms; perfected their ceremonials; and elaborated upon their already intricate mythology. It was the golden age of the Navajo, and it lasted more than a century and a half.

With the Spaniards banished from the land and their settlements near the pueblos destroyed, there was a sixteen-year period of more and lengthier contacts between the Navajos and the Pueblo Indians. Some intermarriage resulted, allowing The People to mine even deeper the riches of Pueblo culture. When the Spaniards returned they had a new name for the Navajos. They still referred to them as *indios bárbaros*, still thought of them as savages. But, observing the Navajo warriors sitting erect upon their ornamented horses—proud, dignified, bold men—the Spanish could not help but temper their contempt with respect and awe. Now they referred to the Navajos as *Los Dueños del Mundo*, the Lords of the Earth.

Lordly they were. Thanks to the brood mares of Spain, every Navajo family owned horses, and young Navajo warriors developed their raiding techniques to a high art. With only a blanket for a saddle, a Navajo warrior could sit a spirited horse as though he were a part of the animal, directing the beast unerringly with the slightest touch of moccasin against flank.

The Navajo raiding technique was to sweep down upon a grazing flock, wave blankets, and wildly shout "ahu, ahu," stampeding the sheep headlong back to their canyon strongholds, where they would melt away unseen. So haughty were these Lords of the Earth that they even took pains not to steal breeding ewes. They wanted to make sure there would be another flock to steal the next year.

Plundering grain fields and melon fields and orchards was equally easy for the bold warriors. The citizens of the four pueblos nearest Navajo territory—Laguna, Isleta, Jemez, and San Ildefonso—stoically came to accept Navajo raids as a way of life. Quite practically, they could see no reason for blood to be spilled over a simple matter of fruits and vegetables, and they knew the Navajos felt the same. So they proposed a deal: leave our fields and field hands alone during the planting and growing seasons, and at harvest time we will set aside a portion especially for you. The Navajos agreed. To this day, in memory of old times and because to an Indian an agreement is an agreement, Navajos are free to help themselves to generous amounts of corn, squash, melons, and beans when those four pueblos celebrate their harvest festivals.

Raiding prowess was not the only benefit the Navajos derived from Spanish horses. The People, now mounted after centuries on foot, could more easily cover distances that formerly had discouraged much commerce across their vast domain. At last they could visit one another with some regularity. As a result their culture developed and spread, and so did their tribal solidarity.

Two great mountain ranges stretch from north to south across Dinetah. The first consists of the Chuska, Lukachukai, and Carrizo mountains along the Arizona–New Mexico border. The Navajos call it the Goods of Value range and look upon it as a huge being, a man, reclining upon the earth with his head pointing south. His head is Chuska Peak and his feet, Beautiful Mountain. The other range, stretching through west central Arizona, is viewed as a woman. The Navajos call it the Pollen range. The woman's head, Navajo Mountain in southern Utah, points north; her body, Black Mesa, stretches southward. Her feet are Balukai Mesa. To The People, inanimate things are often endowed with a sex: Male Rain, Female Rain; Male Corn, Female Corn; Male Cloud, Female Cloud; and Male Mountain, Female Mountain.

So remote and rugged are some crests, slopes, and precipices that even today one has the eerie feeling that his foot just might be the first to tread on a particular spot, his hand the first to touch a particular tree, and his eye the first to behold a particular vista. Surveying one's surroundings from almost any prominence within Dinetah, the very rocks seem to throb with life, and it is easy to believe with The People that all was fashioned according to supernatural plan. To the Navajos, not only the great mountain ranges and spectacular canyons have sacred meaning, but every tree, every weed, and every wildflower as well. Vegetation—the clothing of Changing Woman (Mother Earth)—is the constant manifestation of her awesome presence and is absolutely essential to the harmony of the world. Thus everything in nature, however seemingly trivial, must be accorded utmost respect.

For centuries The People traversed and explored their wild and wondrous homeland on foot; later, during their golden age, on horseback. They assigned names to places. Some were prosaically descriptive, others quite poetic, for The People had the gift of imagery; Sloping White Rock, Two Gray Hills, Willows Coming Out, Tree on Hill, Coiled Mountain, Place of Moonlight Water, Black Rock Standing, Willows Line Out Like Braids, and War God Spring. Their versatile language lent itself to summing up such elaborate descriptions in a single word. For example,

Todanestya means Where Water Runs Like Fingers Out of a Hill.

Over the centuries, The People came to know their vast domain intimately, to know all the sacred places and their legends. They had no written language in which to preserve accounts of their sacred myths. Scattered in small clusters across a territory the size of New Hampshire, Vermont, and Rhode Island combined, they learned their folklore as children sitting in the fire-glow of isolated hogans. They listened to old men recite the ancient tales over the pungent embers of piñon boughs, or they learned them at communal ceremonies.

A Navajo ceremonial, called a Sing, was far more than a religious rite. It was also an opportunity to visit, to trade, to exchange news, to dress up in one's finest clothes and jewelry, and to be his handsomest before his clansmen, his neighbors, and his gods. So it remains today. No advertisement need appear in the Navajo newspaper, no announcement over Gallup's Navajo-language radio station. Somehow—"by moccasin telegraph," the Navajos say—word spreads that there will be a Sing at a certain time and place. From miles around The People come, drawn from their jobs and fields by an unquenchable thirst periodically to refresh their personal and tribal souls. How much more this was true in the old days when their sense of remoteness and aloneness was even more acute.

When Navajo strangers met at a Sing, the first thing they found out was each other's clan. To marry within one's own clan or within one's father's clan was regarded as incestuous, the ugliest of crimes. In the beginning, the legends say, there was but one clan. It divided and subdivided into more than sixty, each with its own legend of how it split off from its mother clan and became its own entity. Most clan names designate localities, suggesting that their origins may have been rooted in geographical groupings. Such names include Bitter Water Clan, Parallel Stream Clan, Standing House Clan, Yucca Blossom Patch Clan, Gray Earth Place Clan, and Red Clay Clan. Other names are equally colorful: Many Goats, Poles Strung Out, Walk Around You, Mountain Rincon, Mud, Red Forehead, Under His Cover, Trail to the Garden.

The Navajo was born into his mother's clan. Members of his father's clan were also relatives but of a subtly different type. A Navajo would describe himself as "born for" his father's clan. Thus, meeting a stranger, he might say "I am Red Forehead born for Bitter Water." On discovering that they were related the two would welcome each other warmly and would perhaps exchange gifts.

The clan, not the biological family, was the most important element of social control. Every clan member was responsible for the crimes and debts of other members, and so it was in the interest of all to prevent wrongdoing. Moreover, every clan was "linked" in an informal way with up to five or six others; perhaps in antiquity they were one. Thus a person's obligations extended not only to his and his father's clansmen but in a less binding degree to members of linked clans as well. This was an important factor in preventing intratribal quarrels and in promoting tribal solidarity. The worst slur one Navajo could make about another was, "He acts as though he had no relatives." By the same token, the ideal of behavior was to "act as though everybody were related to you."

Kinship terminology among The People was equally perplexing to non-Navajos. The Navajo word for "mother" referred also to the mother's sisters and a number of other women. To distinguish his actual mother from the others, a Navajo had to say "she who gave me birth." Similarly, the terms translated as "uncle," "nephew," "cousin," and "niece" referred to relationships far more encompassing than their English equivalents. A Navajo, for example, would refer to his biological uncle as "my nephew" if the uncle happened to be younger than himself, or to an older nephew as "my uncle." "Cousin" referred only to cross-cousins—children of a mother's brother or a father's sister.

Though descent was traced through the mother, the father was head of the immediate biological family. He often had two or more wives, and in most cases they were sisters. Each maintained her separate hogan, usually side by side in the cluster of family dwellings, sheep corrals, and work shelters. Both shared the chores of cooking, weaving, and tending livestock.

Aside from personal items such as clothing, jewelry, and saddles, The People had no conception of private property. Meadow, mountain, stream, and woodland belonged to all The People. A cornfield or peach orchard was respected as the bounty of the man who planted it, but no individual was considered the owner of the land on which it grew. And even though it was regarded as bad manners to cut timber within a mile or so of another's hogan, every Navajo realized that the timber belonged to all The People, just as the Holy Ones had ordained.

This concept enabled The People to continue their seminomadic ways, driving their flocks to the lush mountain heights in the spring to fatten them on grama grass, living under rude shelters of evergreen boughs during the months when Father Sun blessed Mother Earth with his warmth, and returning to their snug hogans when the chill breath of winter swept out of the black regions of the North.

To the People, a hogan was far more than a shelter. The Ant People were responsible for its fundamental design, and the Holy People built the first hogan out of turquoise, white shell, and jet. Navajo myths prescribed the nature of the hogan. It must be five or six sided, with the door facing east to welcome the strengthening rays of the morning sun. Its occupants must deport themselves with women seated on the north side, men on the south, and the male head of the family on the west facing the doorway. The supporting pole on the east side represented Earth Woman; on the south, Mountain Woman; on the west, Water Woman; and on the north, Corn Woman. The head of the family must spread sacred corn pollen on the poles and pray, "Let this be assurance that our hogan will be happy." The dreaded bodies of the dead must be painted with red ochre and removed through a hole broken in the north wall, the direction of evil; and the hogan must be burned to the ground.

For every human activity there was a ritual song, prayer, or action, and each attested to the oneness of man and the universe. The more songs a person knew, the more harmonious, productive, and safe his life would be. The herdsman knew the Owl Song so that his sheep, like the owl, could endure the cold of winter. The raider before setting out on his raid knew how to anoint his arrows with charcoal from a lightning-struck tree. He knew the songs to the Wind People and the Sun People so he could sing them while purifying himself for hours in the sweathouse

—a hole or miniature hogan with heated rocks. The weaver knew the song to Spider Woman, who taught the weaving art to the Holy Ones, who then gave the song to The People. The planter knew the prescribed method of planting corn in the deep hole punched in the ground by his wife (only females dared disturb Mother Earth) and why he should place precisely sixteen kernels in each hill: four for the cutworm, four for the crow, four for the beetle, and four to grow. The traveler knew the songs for a safe journey, or for success if the trip was for trading or for wooing. For every stage in life there was a sacred ritual—for birth, puberty, marriage, and death. For every routine of living there was a prayer—for rising, retiring, and fetching food and water.

The People had an equally long list of "Thou Shalt Nots." Certain animals, coyotes and snakes, among others, must never be killed. Raw meat, most fish, and most water birds must never be eaten. A son's eyes must never look directly into those of his mother-in-law. One must never comb his hair at night. Even in a crowded hogan one must not step over the reclining body of another. All these things were *bahadzid*, "forbidden."

All of nature must be respected for its place in the harmony of the universe. Before the hunter killed the deer, he spoke to him: "I know that your life is as precious as mine, but I must kill you. Come to me, deer, and do not worry. I will eat your flesh, and your life will continue in mine." He made a similar explanation to the pine tree before felling it with his ax. When he butchered a sheep he laid its head to the east, toward Father Sun's hogan, and let some blood from its throat seep into the bosom of Mother Earth.

Guided by the gods themselves in every aspect of his

life, the Navajo had no need for a priest or a policeman or even a chief, in the romantic sense of some warbonneted hierarch. Among The People a central authority would have been superfluous. Families who lived in various geographical locations often joined in communal chores, for instance at sheep shearing time, and frequently one man would emerge as a leader, or headman, for that territory. He was not elected or in any way designated as such but merely deferred to because of his demonstrated wisdom, skill in animal husbandry, oratorical prowess, ceremonial knowledge, or other prestigious traits. His influence was purely persuasive; he possessed no vested authority over the group. Not only was the concept of coercive authority entirely alien to The People, it was regarded as fundamentally indecent. A single individual presuming to make decisions for others would be the object of ridicule. Headmen became headmen not by majority vote but by gradual and unanimous consent, and they assumed the role humbly and reluctantly.

Restrained in their behavior by their customs, by their obligations to fellow clansmen, and by mythological taboos, The People were nonetheless the Lords of the Earth, at home in Dinetah.

THE NAVAJO WAY

"IN BEAUTY MAY I WALK"

CHAPTER SEVEN

A Navajo girl was ill. Let us call her Tall Woman's daughter. Tall Woman knew, of course, that illness had a supernatural cause. Somehow her daughter had gotten out of harmony with the universe. Perhaps she had stepped on a snake or insulted a bear. Or maybe the girl had harbored evil thoughts against another. Whatever the cause, Tall Woman discussed her daughter's symptoms with her, talked the matter over with her husband, and consulted her relatives. Finally it was agreed. Tall Woman must hold a Sing for her daughter.

For every physical or mental disorder, the Holy Ones had provided an appropriate cure. The People called them "Ways." Mountain Top Way removed the bad effects of bears. Beauty Way cured any malady caused by snakes. Flint Way restored lost vitality. Big Star Way banished bad dreams. Night Way allayed mental anguish. Enemy Way removed the evil caused by contact with alien people. There were dozens more, each a distinct ceremony with a distinct purpose.

Tall Woman had to consult a diagnostician who would determine, by divination, the cause of the girl's particular ailment. That done, a singer had to be found who knew the proper healing ritual. It would be most unusual for a singer to know more than a few ceremonials. Night Way, for example, over a period of nine days and nights, included 576 songs; 4 sand paintings; several dances; and carefully prescribed usages for rattles, masks, and male and female prayer sticks.

Each singer specialized in one Way, which took him nearly a lifetime to learn. He began as an apprentice studying at the feet of an older singer with whom he went to live. Over the years he paid the old scholar for the sacred knowledge with gifts of sheep, or perhaps with skins of deer killed without bloodshed—smothered to death with corn pollen. The skins would be used for ceremonial masks. He paid for the information because ceremonial knowledge, unlike tangible goods, was considered personal property. In fifteen or twenty years, after the student had mastered all the songs and rituals, after he had assisted his tutor in the ceremony many times so that he could perform it without the slightest flaw, and after he had had the rite performed over him to make sure he could stand its great power—only then did he become a singer. He would never flaunt his knowledge, but the ritual would be his most valuable possession. He would be considered a wealthy man in the only sense that The People considered riches an asset.

Having located a singer and agreed upon a fee, Tall Woman and her clansmen had to put aside mutton and fry-bread to feed the great crowd that would come to the Sing, and had to haul enough firewood to warm them at night. To be stingy in this responsibility would insult the gods and destroy the efficacy of the ceremony. Tall Woman knew that many would attend, and without urging. Though always held specifically for the benefit of one individual, all who attended a Sing benefited greatly.

Each ceremony was a legend told in song and symbol concerning some episode in the ancient evolution of The People. Enemy Way recounted the exploits of the Hero Twins, who slew a number of monsters threatening The People. The ceremony destroyed the ghosts of those alien monsters and thus the ghosts of all aliens with whom the patient might have come in contact.

Each ceremonial lasted one, three, five, or nine days and required one or more sand paintings. The Navajos learned the art of sand painting in shared ceremonies with the Pueblo Indians but, like weaving and other arts adapted to their own use, they raised it to a new level of perfection; sand painting has come to be regarded as strictly Navajo. More precise students refer to them as dry paintings, since in addition to colored sand for their designs the painters used pulverized plants and other materials—dried larkspur blossoms to make blue, cornmeal for white, corn pollen for yellow, charcoal (from a lightning-struck tree) for black, and various mixtures to make other hues.

In their stylized simplicity the paintings reflected deep meanings, as beautiful and profound as any indigenous art in the Americas. They pictured rivers, fields, rainbows, clouds, Holy People, plants, and animals. The singer trickled the loose sand through the crook of his forefinger onto an unwounded buckskin, or onto the floor of the ceremonial hogan, since the paintings could be twelve feet or so across. No painting lasted more than a day. The painting was begun at first light, finished by afternoon, used ceremonially, and destroyed before nightfall. In most ceremonies the patient sat cross-legged on the painting, absorbing its awesome power.

During the ceremony the singer chanted his repetitious songs, at times to the hypnotic accompaniment of a drum of unwounded buckskin stretched over a ceramic pot. Masked dancers performed their staccato steps. Within the ceremonial hogan every color, every gesture, every item used in the rite was replete with meaning. All present surrendered their minds and bodies totally to the invisible forces surrounding them, willingly mesmerized by the lyrical litanies of the sacred chants. For example, Dawn Boy's song:

In the house of long life, there I wander.
In the house of happiness, there I wander.
Beauty before me, with it I wander.
Beauty behind me, with it I wander.
Beauty below me, with it I wander.
Beauty above me, with it I wander.
Beauty all around me, with it I wander.
In old age traveling, with it I wander.
On the beautiful trail I am, with it I wander.

Song of the Earth Spirit:

It is lovely indeed, it is lovely indeed.
I, I am the spirit within the earth.
The feet of the earth are my feet.

The legs of the earth are my legs.
The strength of the earth is my strength.
The thoughts of the earth are my thoughts.
The voice of the earth is my voice.
The feather of the earth is my feather.
All that belongs to the earth belongs to me.
All that surrounds the earth surrounds me.
I, I am the sacred words of the earth.
It is lovely indeed, it is lovely indeed.

Night Way Prayer:

In beauty may I walk.
All day long may I walk.
Through the returning seasons may I walk.
Beautifully will I possess again.
Beautifully birds.
Beautifully joyful birds.
On the trail marked with pollen may I walk.
With grasshoppers about my feet may I walk.
With dew about my feet may I walk.
With beauty may I walk.
With beauty all around me may I walk.
In old age wandering on a trail of beauty,
   lively may I walk.
In old age wandering on a trail of beauty,
   living again may I walk.
It is finished in beauty.
It is finished in beauty.

Though each ceremonial myth was a separate and distinct story, characters often recurred. The Hero Twins appeared in many ceremonials; so did *Yeibichai*, the Talking God of the East, maternal grandfather of all the *Yei*, the Saints. And *Xascelbai*, the Water Sprinkler, god of rain and snow, who brought happiness and mirth. Plants and animals appeared as sentient beings—Red Ant People, Cat Tail People, and Cutting Reed People.

Familiar characters reappeared in more than one legend because each ceremonial was an elaboration of an incident in one central legend, the Navajo Origin Myth. The ceremonial which had as its theme the Origin Myth was Blessing Way, the only ceremonial held as a preventive rather than as a cure.

The legend reveals a cosmogony as complex and profound as that of any of the great Oriental or Western religions. A closer look at it, therefore, would be useful.

In the beginning The People's ancestors lived in the First World, a world of darkness inhabited only by six beings: First Man, son of Night and Blue Sunset; First Woman, daughter of Daybreak and Yellow Sunset; Fire God, son of Comet; Coyote, Child of Dawn; Salt Woman, daughter of Water Woman and Mountain Man; and *Begochiddy*, who was both man and woman, offspring of the Sun. They dwelt around the great rock, the Mountain Around Which Moving Was Done. Encircling it were four sacred mountains. This great rock was also referred to as Encircled Mountain, White Corn Mountain, Long Life Mountain, and Mountain of Beauty. The four sacred mountains are visible and identifiable as the boundaries of Dinetah. Encircled Mountain, however, was as mystical as it was physical. Though some have identified it as El Huerfano Peak, above Chaco Canyon, that can only be a symbol of it, because Encircled Mountain cannot be contained in any limited time-space dimension; it will exist in the world beyond the present world.

The First World was destroyed by fire. In the Second

World various plants and animals appeared, including the sacred plants of corn, beans, tobacco, and squash. This world was destroyed by water.

In the Third World wind appeared, the breath of life. Also streams (male and female), water creatures, birds, and lightning. There was as yet no daylight, but the sacred mountains shed light dimly, "like a valley in starlight." Many adventures occurred in the Third World, including the temporarily disastrous separation of the sexes. Each sex, in vanity, had supposed it could get along without the other. Like the Second World, this world was destroyed by a great flood.

The Fourth World also was flooded, and First Man and First Woman led the prototypes of all beings, creatures, plants, and rocks to the present world, the Fifth World. The actual place of emergence has been listed variously as Spirit Lake, Silver Lake, or Island Lake in the mountains of southern Colorado.

The story of their emergence accounted not only for The People's arrival in the present world but also for their evolution as human beings. In the First World, from Fire God, they received the heat of their bodies; from the Wind of the Second World, their breath. White shell formed their knees; zigzag lightning, their legs; straight lightning, their tongues; white corn, their teeth; black corn, their eyebrows; daybreak, their flesh; darkness, their hair; thunder, their voices; and rain, their tears. They emerged as Beings Created from Everything, The People.

They were also composites of good and evil. Changing Woman, the Earth Mother, deposited in the back of each person's head a speck no larger than a grain of sand, which accounts for the bad dreams, evil thoughts, and mistakes people make. When they die it is this "evil spirit," the *chindi*, which remains on earth to haunt the unwary; their good spirit ascends to the Sun, the reservoir of life.

Changing Woman was born in the Fourth World at the foot of Encircled Mountain, the child of Darkness and Dawn. First Man and First Woman nourished her with sun rays, clouds, dew, and the elements of the three preceding worlds—fire, air, and water. When she came of age, a Blessing Way was held for her.

After the emergence The People were troubled by a great many monsters. Changing Woman sat four days in the sunlight, receiving his rays, absorbing the virility of Father Sun, and in nine months she gave birth to the Hero Twins. When they were twelve years old they decided to go find their father, the Sun, and ask his advice on getting rid of the monsters. They stepped off the primordial earth onto a cloud, thence across the arched path of Rainbow Man to the House of the Sun. The Sun received them. One twin he named Monster Slayer, and gave him lightning arrows; the other he named Child of the Water, and to him he gave wisdom. They returned to earth at the time of the May moon (which divides the year into half summer, half winter) and rid the earth of the monsters in exploits of bravery and wonder.

And so to Tall Woman's ceremonial hogan The People came and listened to the lyrical beauty of the songs that would cure her daughter, watched in awe the masked dancers, and heard once again the adventures of their gods from the eternal cosmos reassuring them that all was in order. The earth and all its creatures and plants

and streams and rainbows were one, the ultimate beauty.
Returning to their hogans they could sing:

> *I will be happy forever,*
> *Nothing will hinder me.*
> *With beauty before me I walk.*
> *With beauty behind me I walk.*
> *With beauty below me I walk.*
> *With beauty above me I walk.*
> *With beauty all around me I walk.*
> *My words will be beautiful!*
> *My words will be beautiful!*

THE AGE
OF TREATIES

CHAPTER EIGHT

Not the lyrical poetry of Navajo ceremonial songs, not the ethical patterns of Navajo culture, but simply the bold efficiency of Navajo raiding parties was the characteristic of The People which Brig. Gen. Stephen Watts Kearny considered of immediate and pressing concern in the late summer of 1846.

Listening to the strident reports of the New Mexicans who arrived daily from their Rio Grande settlements to pay obeisance to their courtly conqueror, General Kearny most assuredly heard nothing to suggest that the Navajos were capable of feelings or instincts any more profound than filling their bellies on other people's corn or driving off other people's sheep. Nor did it likely occur to the general that the building he now occupied in Santa Fe—

the Palace of the Governors, in which he graciously received the New Mexicans' pledges of fealty—was built with the forced labor of Indian slaves. That sort of thing was not often discussed in proper Santa Fe *salas*. With a few notable exceptions, the feeling on the American frontier in the year 1846 was that the Indians possessed no human dignity that any white man was obliged to respect. That feeling grew deeper and uglier in the years to come.

On September 25, General Kearny left Santa Fe, anxious to get to California to certify America's conquest of Mexico. To be in command at Santa Fe he designated Col. Alexander William Doniphan, the tall, redheaded commander of a regiment of Missouri Mounted Volunteers (who had elected him their leader). The general's departing orders to Doniphan were to take a force of chosen men into Navajo country and wring from the marauding tribesmen a pledge that they would give up their predatory ways and live in peace forever.

Kearny had already sent two detachments from Doniphan's regiment to take up outposts along the favorite raiding routes of the Navajos in the west and the Utes in the north. One detachment was at Cebolleta, about sixty miles west of Albuquerque; the other at Abiquiu, approximately sixty miles northwest of Santa Fe.

Neither detachment was notably successful. A week after the troops (three companies) arrived at Cebolleta, a band of Navajos brazenly raided the Rio Grande villages of Tomé and Valencia south of Albuquerque and stole five thousand sheep. If the garrison at Cebolleta was ineffective on that count, however, the soldiers did achieve one result of far-reaching value. They became friendly with a man who lived nearby whom the New Mexicans knew as Antonio Sandoval. His own people called him *Keshgoli*, Crooked Foot.

Crooked Foot was a headman in a band of Navajos known to their fellow tribesmen as *Dineanaih*, The People Who Are Enemies. These were the renegade Navajos who had embraced Christianity, or claimed they had, and cast their lot with the Spaniards. Antonio Sandoval was Crooked Foot's Christian name. The number of Dineanaih was estimated at fifty to four hundred, which only proved that nobody actually knew how many there were. They lived on the very edge of Dinetah on the western slopes of the Navajos' sacred mountain of the South, Mount Taylor.

Doniphan planned to carry out General Kearny's orders by sending the detachments bivouacked at Cebolleta and Abiquiu into Navajo country by two different routes. He, with a third column, would move southwest from Santa Fe and rendezvous with the others at a place called *Ojo del Oso*, Bear Springs. The site, a favorite Navajo gathering place located about fifteen miles east of the present Gallup, New Mexico, was a lush and level plain where clear water bubbled from the earth beneath a great cottonwood tree. It would later become the site of a military post. The People would not be pleased when that occurred, for to them it was a holy place. But by that time they would be too weary to weep.

Alexander Doniphan planned to enact his treaty at Ojo del Oso in the approaching winter of 1846. All three of his military columns had instructions to round up en route as many Navajo "chiefs" as they could find. Should that prove difficult, the soldiers were authorized "to chastise the Navajos wherever they appeared hostile." In the American experience an Indian always seemed more reasonable about signing treaties if a knife was held to his throat. Doniphan wanted to end this diplomatic affair as quickly as possible; he was anxious to be on his way down the Rio Grande to join in the fight with the Mexicans. The colonel had not yet gotten the news that Mexico City had already fallen and the war was over.

The troops at Cebolleta were only six days' march from Ojo del Oso. It would take Doniphan and the Abiquiu units weeks to get there. One of the men of the Cebolleta command, a captain named Reid, saw an opportunity to use the extra time to spare the Navajos possible American punitive measures. He suggested that he escort the renegade Sandoval and a small peace party of thirty men into Navajo country to try to persuade the chieftains to go willingly to Santa Fe and treat with the Americans at their headquarters. Reid's commanding officer at Cebolleta agreed that it was worth a try.

After an arduous march across the chill and rugged heights of the Continental Divide, Reid and his party reached Ojo del Oso. Sandoval had had the good fortune to hear about a Sing being held in the vicinity and so had no trouble rounding up a crowd. Before long several thousand Navajos had gathered at the spring on their colorful ponies to have a look at the New Men. The warriors accepted Reid at his word, that he had come in peace. They fed their white guests roasted mutton ribs and even put on a show for them, impressing at least one of the soldiers with "a sight unequalled in display of horsemanship."

One of the Navajo elders who came to greet Reid was a

sagacious old headman of extraordinary dignity who was held in great admiration and respect by his clansmen and neighbors. He called himself Narbona. The People had another name for him, after their fashion of honoring one's personal traits; they called him Man Speaking Peace. Narbona was about eighty years old and crippled with rheumatism but nonetheless regal in bearing. One American trooper could not help likening the stately Indian to George Washington.

With Sandoval as interpreter, Reid explained his purpose to Narbona. The Indian nodded. He consulted with some of the others, and told Reid they would be glad to go to Santa Fe and talk peace with the New Men. Reid sent a courier galloping off to Doniphan with the happy report, bade a pleasant farewell to the Navajos, and headed back to Cebolleta. Narbona did not bother to tell Reid that he and his colleagues, as Navajos, spoke only for themselves; he assumed this was understood. Indeed, just before Reid left, Narbona gave him a bit of friendly advice. He told the captain to keep a sharp eye on the army stables at Cebolleta; he had heard some of the young Navajos talking. When Reid returned, he discovered half the horse herd missing.

Reid had not rested many days in Cebolleta when a dispatch arrived from Colonel Doniphan. There would be no treaty negotiations in Santa Fe. The original plan would be executed as ordered—a three-pronged expedition into Navajo country from Cebolleta, Abiquiu, and Santa Fe, culminating in a parley at Ojo del Oso with Doniphan in charge. The colonel, it seems, would brook no delay in getting to the Mexican border. He and his Missourians had volunteered to fight Mexicans, not to powwow with redskins. Reid's friendly meeting with Narbona and the others had been a waste of time.

Late in December the three columns (330 soldiers) straggled into Ojo del Oso. They found waiting for them about 500 Navajos. Narbona was there, and there were other faces familiar to Reid. Doniphan tried to explain to the Navajos, through Sandoval, that the United States of America now owned the land called New Mexico and was obliged to protect its inhabitants from Indian incursions. If the Navajos continued to raid the Mexicans' flocks and fields the Americans would have no alternative except "to prosecute a war against them."

One can only guess how much of Doniphan's expostulations the Navajos understood. Every sentence had to be translated twice; Sandoval spoke Navajo and Spanish, but not English. And the very concepts of territory, nationhood, and treaty which the Americans took for granted were alien to anything in the Navajos' experience.

One thing that the Navajos apparently did grasp— assuming the accuracy of both the chronicler and the retranslation—left them understandably perplexed. Doniphan had warned that if the Indians continued to raid Mexican ranches, the Americans would shoot the Indians. On hearing that, a bemused Navajo headman named Long Earrings asked if he might speak. He simply could not understand, he said, how the Americans could object to the Navajos making war on the Mexicans. Weren't they themselves currently engaged in the same thing? "This is our war," the Indian is quoted as saying. "We have more right to complain of you for interfering in our war than you have to quarrel with us for continuing a war we had begun long before you got here."

Narbona, Long Earrings, and several other headmen sighed and put their Xs on Doniphan's paper, thereby promising "permanent peace, mutual trust and friendship."

How the Navajos truly regarded the Doniphan treaty is not recorded; Americans in Santa Fe sniffed in derision. "It is here thought," wrote a Santa Fe correspondent to the *St. Louis Weekly Reveille*, that the Navajos "will continue to steal sheep and commit other outrages until they are well whipped a few times. . . ."

Navajo raids in fact did continue unchecked. But were the men who had signed the treaty responsible for them? United States officials and citizens never could realize— apparently they never tried—that unlike American democracy, Navajo democracy was so real that no one man could speak for any other. To the New Mexicans it was the Navajos, collectively, who deserved punishment. If the "chiefs" couldn't keep their subjects in line was that not further evidence of Indian perfidy and wildness? Unfortunately, the feeling prevalent in Santa Fe was the feeling dominant in America's highest official circles, and it was destined to find expression in a macabre cliché: "The only good Indian is a dead Indian."

Ten months after the Doniphan treaty was signed and discarded, a battalion of soldiers left Santa Fe with two months' provisions, aiming to give the Navajos a trouncing they wouldn't forget. It promised to be good sport. As an observer reported, "nearly every man left drunk." The column trudged deep into Dinetah and even probed six miles into Canyon de Chelly, the labyrinthine Navajo stronghold.

They didn't see a single Navajo. How could you make

good Indians out of live ones if you couldn't find them? One official report from Santa Fe to Washington put the problem in a pathetically amusing light: "Our troops are of no earthly account. They cannot catch a single Indian. A dragoon mounted will weigh 225 pounds. Their horses are all as poor as carrion. The Indians have nothing but their bows and arrows and their ponies are as fleet as deer. Cipher it up."

Col. E. W. R. Newby, the new military governor at Santa Fe, was personally aware of the problem. He himself had once led a column of troops into Dinetah and after a few desultory skirmishes had concluded another perfunctory treaty with any headmen willing to sign. He saw clearly the futility of traditional military operations against the elusive Dineh. Ciphering it up, he issued a proclamation on March 27, 1848, authorizing the New Mexicans to form their own bands of civilian irregulars and make reprisal raids on the Navajos "as the only means of protection remaining."

Newby must have been aware that a great many New Mexicans made very good livelihoods by raiding in Navajo country. From what source did he suppose came the endless supply of Indians sold daily as slaves in every New Mexican marketplace? Newby's edict gave official sanction to the merciless depredations that the well-armed and enterprising New Mexican traders had been conducting for decades. The frontier was never more lawless.

The following year Congress took the responsibility for treating with Indians away from the War Department and gave it to the brand new Department of Interior. In July, James S. Calhoun, a Georgian, arrived in Santa Fe as the first Indian Agent. Calhoun had fought beside Gen. Zachary Taylor in the war with Mexico and was a fellow Whig. Appointment as Indian Agent was his political reward when Taylor became president. Calhoun immediately decided to try his hand at treaty making. In the classic thought-pattern of the day, he felt that the Navajos would be more amenable if first intimidated by American military might. Give The People a whiff of grape, as it were.

With Bvt. Lt. Col. John Macrae Washington, who had succeeded Newby as military governor, Agent Calhoun started for Navajo country. He and Washington rode at the head of a column of 175 men. The command included infantry, cavalry, artillery, and a special force of 54 Pueblo Indian volunteers from six pueblos, who were gleeful about the opportunity for revenge and grateful for the protection of allies. As usual, Sandoval went along as guide and interpreter.

The imposing force dragged its clattering howitzers through the ravines of Chaco Canyon and on August 30 reached the green valley of Tunicha. Navajo scouts, unseen by the soldiers, had observed every mile of the march. As soon as the soldiers made camp, several hundred mounted Navajos appeared and made overtures of friendship, only to watch the soldiers casually picket their horses in The People's ripe cornfields. The Dineh said nothing.

The next day more Navajos arrived. Among them was the venerable Narbona, who lived nearby, so racked with pain he could barely sit a horse. Narbona and the other headmen listened as Agent Calhoun explained—through Sandoval, whom The People despised—that the Americans aimed to proceed all the way to Canyon de Chelly to enact a great treaty. Calhoun apparently believed that if he were ever to find the "big chief" of the Navajos, he certainly would be in the storied canyon stronghold. Narbona said he was not physically able to make the trip but that he agreed to the terms of the treaty and would ask a like-minded friend, Armijo, to go in his stead.

Sandoval paraded arrogantly before them, explaining the treaty to the assembled Navajo warriors. Meanwhile, an American soldier moved over to Colonel Washington and said he recognized a horse one of the Navajos was riding; it was his, he said, stolen months before. Lt. J. H. Simpson, a member of the force, made careful notes of what followed.

Colonel Washington demanded that the Navajo give up the horse. The Navajo refused. His comrades likewise refused to take it from him. Had Colonel Washington understood the Navajo conscience or the Navajo clan, he would have known that he was asking them to engage in unconscionable meddling and even potential fratricide. Besides, horse stealing had been a mutual practice of both Mexicans and Navajos for years. The very horse in question, they told him, had changed hands many times. The animal would not be given up. The Navajos were adamant.

So was Colonel Washington. "Give back the horse," he said evenly, "or we'll fire." Not an Indian moved. "Seize the horse!" shouted the colonel. "Seize *any* horse!" An officer lunged toward a Navajo mount. As he did, every warrior wheeled and galloped off. Muskets barked. Cannons opened fire on the fleeing Indians.

One Navajo fell dead—Narbona. Many others were wounded, at least six mortally.

The expeditionary force eventually did reach its goal, Canyon de Chelly. It penetrated the awesome gorge nine miles, following a trail of smoke as frightened parents gathered up their children, fired their hogans, and cowered in the canyon's hidden recesses. "It was somewhat exciting," wrote Lt. Simpson, "to observe the huts of the enemy, one after another, springing up into smoke and flame and their owners scampering off in flight." (Even as the owners' grandparents had once scampered to the bloody grotto of Cañon del Muerto.) The Americans did not overlook the opportunity to stock up on food and fodder from the abandoned fields.

Indian Agent Calhoun eventually succeeded in getting his treaty. He gave some hoes and bright cloth to two Navajo males designated as "Head Chief" and "Second Chief," in gratitude for their Xs on yet another piece of paper. This he dutifully sent to Washington for solemn ratification by the Senate of the United States, in order to, in the words of the treaty, "secure the permanent prosperity and happiness of said [Navajo] Indians."

Across the mesas and meadows of Dinetah the story spread of what had happened that August day in the valley of Tunicha. The New Men had offered The People peace while stealing their corn. They had shot down the well-loved Narbona after he had agreed to their terms. They had slaughtered at least six other Navajos without cause. The New Men were no different from the Mexicans; they were no different from the Spaniards. They were enemies.

FORT DEFIANCE

CHAPTER NINE

The Dineh lashed back. Out of canyon and gorge horse hoofs thundered from the eastern edge of Dinetah toward the ranches and pueblos of the enemy. War whoops chilled the countryside at Cebolleta, La Pugarita, Abiquiu, Cubero, and Corrales. Terror-stricken *pastores* abandoned flock after flock to the raiders, fleeing in utter terror of the silent vengeance of the Navajo arrow fletched with eagle feathers and engraved with a lightning bolt to make its flight swift and true. Under the noses of the white soldiers, the raiders struck at the pueblos of San Ildefonso, Santo Domingo, and Santa Ana. Had not Pueblo warriors accompanied the New Men on their murderous march to the Tunicha?

Although the Rio Grande villagers were generally horrified by the Navajo predations, one group among them cheered every Indian raid. To unscrupulous New Mexican traders, the Navajo uprising produced a double-barreled boom in the slave market. In the first place, they could blame the Navajos for their own slave raids against the pueblos. In addition, they could count on official government approval of vigilante "reprisals" against the Navajos, which was simply another name for slave raids. An average Navajo child aged five to fifteen brought as much as $200 on the market, and literally thousands were sold.

The renegade Sandoval, as one might expect, had no scruples about selling his brethren into slavery. Unfortunately for Sandoval, he was still an Indian and could not command anywhere near the market price for his captives. A frontier missionary visiting in Cebolleta in March of 1851 reported that Sandoval sold an eighteen-year-old Navajo youth for a paltry thirty dollars. Several days later Sandoval showed up in Santa Fe with "eighteen captives, a quantity of stock and several scalps," according to James Calhoun, who, that same month, was promoted to civil governor and superintendent of Indian affairs for the territory.

With an official wink at Sandoval's outrages, Calhoun issued his first gubernatorial executive order, a directive authorizing reprisals against the Navajos by New Mexican vigilantes. Colonel Newby had done the same thing three years earlier, unleashing an orgy of lawlessness; Calhoun went a step further. He also encouraged the Pueblo Indians to join in the hunt, cynically fomenting intertribal war. "The Navajos," Calhoun instructed the leaders of every pueblo, "must be exterminated or so chastised as to prevent their coming into or near your pueblo."

The New Mexican frontier was never more turbulent than during those first years following Mexico's defeat. The California gold discovery in 1848 loosed a flood of westering humanity across the plains. By 1850 weekly stage lines plied the Santa Fe Trail. In 1851 sixty thousand people passed through the territory. In the wagon tracks of the gold seekers wallowed the inevitable transient scum—camp followers, profiteers, outlaws, gamblers, and fugitives. The Indian, who ranked in status several cuts below the meanest white, could not have been much impressed by the onslaught of "civilization."

Just what status the Navajo did hold in America remained something of a mystery. The Treaty of Guadalupe Hidalgo, which ended the Mexican war, provided that all the Mexican citizens in the territory could if they wished become American citizens. This included the Pueblo Indians but specifically excluded the "wild Indians," the Navajos. On the other hand, America assumed responsibility for Navajo raids across the Mexican border. Thus The People were officially neither citizens nor aliens, but merely a troublesome species of local fauna.

Gold fever, a California malady in 1849, spread to New Mexico in the early 1850s. Prospectors uncovered a small vein in the Ortiz Mountains, between Santa Fe and Albuquerque, and overnight all the old treasure myths dormant since the days of the Conquistadores were revived in frontier saloons. Many a sun-dimmed pioneer eye covetously scanned the peaks of Navajo country to the west and imagined mountains of riches there for the taking. It was all a mirage, of course; but who could be sure unless the Indians were "taken care of" and the land made safe for settlers?

New Mexican ranchers discovered they already had a gold mine right out in their pastures; the exploding California population hungered for all the mutton New Mexico could provide. In 1850 a daring herdsman named William Angney drove a flock of six thousand New Mexico sheep across the Mojave Desert to California mining camps, proving that it could be done. Others followed. If the westward sheep drives did not match the eastward cattle drives in glamor or publicity, they more than made up for it in profits. Sheep fetched eight dollars a head in California. In New Mexico they cost a dollar a head. Or, if stolen from the Navajos whose flocks were huge, hardy, and tended by women and children, they cost not a cent.

It would be hard to imagine a civil government less able than that of the New Mexico Territory to deal with the wanton lawlessness of the period. The first civil governor, Charles Bent of Taos, who had been appointed by General Kearny, was slain in his home January 19, 1847. The murder was part of a wider plot patterned after the Indians' successful 1680 revolt, which drove out the Spanish, and it was hatched in the same nest of resistance, the Taos Pueblo. But it had a far different outcome. American soldiers stormed the pueblo, killed 150 insurgents and hanged 14 captives.

After Bent's assassination, New Mexico's leadership at nearly every governmental level seemed to change practically with the seasons. As one frustrated territorial delegate lamented in a report to Washington, "For the last three years we have suffered under the paralyzing effects of a government undefined and doubtful in its character . . . industry and enterprise are paralyzed, and discontent and confusion prevail throughout the land . . . we have neither the means nor any adopted plan by government for the education of the rising generation. . . ." Education certainly was a problem; there were only eight schoolteachers in the entire territory, and half the population was illiterate.

The new military governor of New Mexico in the spring of 1851 was Col. Edwin Vose Sumner, a professional soldier who had risen through the officer ranks with distinction. Sumner had not been in Santa Fe a month before he made the same assessment as had each of his predecessors: "No permanent peace can exist with the Indians and no treaty will be regarded by them until they have been made to feel the power of our arms." The American military seemed to have a one-track mind.

Sumner mustered a massive force for a spring campaign against the Navajos. It required forty wagons to haul all the equipment. With trumpets blaring and guidons snapping in the May breeze, the troops made for The People's heartland, Canyon de Chelly.

About six miles north of the present Window Rock, Arizona, the column arrived at a lush rincon nestled among red sandstone hills where the grass grew tall and cool springs bubbled. The Mexicans had named the place *Cañon Bonito*, Pretty Canyon. The Navajos were more precise; they called it *Tsehotsohih*, Meadow Between the Rocks. It was one of their shrines. The stream bottom glittered with bits of turquoise and white shell tossed as offerings. Here and there stood cairns three to five feet high made of stones, twigs, and bits of turquoise and shell. They were a Navajo version of roadside chapels. Petitioners built them over the years, uttering such prayers as:

Placing rocks, Male One.
Placing rocks, Female One.
Everywhere I go
May I, myself, have happiness.
Everywhere my relatives go
May they have their happiness.

Colonel Sumner selected the spot as a base camp. Leaving his wagons, he took a mounted detachment and headed for Canyon de Chelly. The troop penetrated the gorge fifteen miles, the farthest yet. But each night campfires glowed ominously on the lofty ledges above, and an occasional arrow whistled down from the heights. Sumner decided to pull out while he could.

Except as a sightseeing trip the expedition could scarcely be considered an epic success. But Sumner's military mind took careful note of that grassy meadow. What an ideal spot for an army post! Of course, the place was 210 miles west of Albuquerque. Logistics problems were obvious; no American outpost was that remote from any frontier. But a U.S. fort standing brazenly in the very camp of the enemy, Sumner reckoned, would surely present a wrenching psychological affront as well as a bold military barrier to the Navajos. Sumner decided to leave a cadre behind to build it. He picked an apt name for the post: Fort Defiance.

THE FIRST
RESERVATION

"MY PEOPLE ARE ALL CRYING"

CHAPTER TEN

The People watched in outraged silence from the red cliffs above as the rude buildings of Fort Defiance took shape in their scared meadow.

The raids stopped. A delegation of Navajo headmen from the Canyon Bonito area journeyed to Santa Fe and confronted Colonel Sumner. He told them that Fort Defiance would remain and that the soldiers garrisoned there "would prevent them from raising a single field of grain unless they remained at peace." He also told them they would have to return all the livestock they had stolen since the territory became part of the United States.

The absurdity of the second demand was equalled only by the official list of stolen livestock itself. When word got out that the army was compiling such a list, Mexican ranchers trooped in from miles around. They reported their losses with a straight face, and an army clerk solemnly recorded each claim. The grand total was: 453,293 sheep; 12,887 mules; 7,050 horses; and 31,581 cattle. That would have meant that every Navajo man, woman, and child was the proud owner of an average of 35 head of stolen livestock. The army stuck by the figures.

From time to time The People did return herds of stolen animals to the Fort Defiance corrals. One reason for their compliance was that the civilian agent stationed there was at last someone who respected the Navajos as people. His name was Henry Linn Dodge. The Navajos called him *Biee Lichii*, Red Shirt; his usual attire was a red flannel shirt stuffed into blue cavalry trousers. Dodge had been an army captain and in fact had been a member of the expedition that resulted in the death of Narbona. But he left the Army and went to live among The People. He took a Navajo wife and settled down near the eastern approach to Washington Pass, named by the Anglos for the leader of that ill-fated expedition. Appointed agent at Fort Defiance, Dodge saddled his horse and rode alone among The People, making a one-man reconnaissance of all of Dinetah. He also brought to the post a Mexican silversmith, Juan Anea, who taught The People his craft. Before long they had infused a distinctively Navajo flavor into their work so that it became an art style of its own.

The Navajos who had agreed to do so had ceased their raids, but the New Mexicans had not. On January 27, 1852, a group of Navajos, no doubt encouraged by their friend Red Sleeves, went to Santa Fe to complain. Among them was Armijo, the faithful friend of old Narbona who had witnessed the signing of the Calhoun treaty.

The chief agent at Santa Fe, John Greiner, told the group that it was the Navajos who had not kept their word, that New Mexicans on the lower Rio Grande had just lately complained of raids. Armijo stepped forward:

My people are all crying the same way. Three of our chiefs now sitting before you mourn for their children, who have been taken from their homes by the Mexicans. More than 200 of our children have been carried off [since the Americans came] and we know not where they are. The Mexicans have lost but few children in comparison with what they have stolen from us. . . . From the time of Colonel Newby we have been trying to get our children back. . . . Eleven times have we given up our captives, only once have they given us ours. My people are yet crying for the children they have lost. . . . Is it American justice that we must give up everything and receive nothing?

For two years the New Mexican frontier remained relatively calm. Then, in the summer of 1855, Agent Dodge was told to pass the word to the Navajos that there would have to be another treaty. Congress had enacted the Indian Appropriation Law, which required a specific boundary to be established for a Navajo reservation. Its size, according to instructions from Washington received by the new civil governor, David Meriwether, should be sufficient to give each family "a farm containing from, say, 20 to 60 acres, according to the number of persons in such family." Until that time the Indian reservation system, the time-worn administrative procedure that had swindled unto death so many proud Indian nations of the East, had not been applied to the Navajos. "Civilization" was drawing ominously close.

Dodge arranged a parley for July 18 at Laguna Negra,

14 miles north of Fort Defiance. Meriwether explained that the Navajos would have a specific and inviolate piece of property containing 7,000 square miles. Of that total, some 125 square miles were suitable for cultivation.

Meriwether produced a map. The People knew their land, even from this strange eagle's-eye view. They saw that it was a mere fraction of their traditional Dinetah and that it did not include any of their own boundary markers, the four sacred mountains of East, South, West, and North. This was pointed out to Meriwether.

He said feebly that the reservation did contain a mountain that he had heard was revered by the Navajos. He pointed to a peak among the Carrizo Mountains, Mount Polonia, today's Pastora Peak. Meriwether said that he had "hoped that this one sacred mountain would be sufficient."

The Navajos, of course, signed the treaty. They had no alternative.

Back in Santa Fe, the dusty streets where sleepy *peones* had once idled away endless lonely hours were bustling with new life. It was 1855, and the West was opening up. Sheep drives to California were at their peak, the supply was not nearly equal to the demand, and new settlers were arriving.

"New limits should be established for the Navajos," proclaimed an editorial in the *Santa Fe Weekly Gazette* three months and a day after the treaty was signed, "so as to give more room for our citizens to graze their stock."

It was the handwriting on the adobe wall. The pattern that had begun with Cotton Mather's pilgrims clearing the woods of Pequots "to make room for a better growth" had finally spread all the way to the Continental Divide.

Never in their existence had the Navajos been confronted with the concept of an arbitrary boundary, a property line. By what strange reasoning could a being presume to claim ownership of the earth? To make matters worse, the one person who might help them comprehend the incomprehensible, Henry Linn Dodge, was gone. Red Shirt, the white Indian agent who had lived like a Navajo, died like one. On November 19, 1856, while hunting south of his adopted Dinetah, a band of Apaches ambushed Dodge and killed him.

For three and a half years The People seethed within the artificial confines of their reservation while New Mexican stockmen raided their flocks incessantly to supply the California trade. Outrages against the Navajos were commonplace. In February of 1858, a gang of drunken New Mexicans waylaid a Navajo man and wife on the road from Albuquerque and killed the woman. In May, a mob from Abiquiu claiming Navajos had stolen some animals rushed onto the reservation, thirsting for blood, and slaughtered the first five Indians they found.

Another slaughter occurred on May 29. The officer in command of Fort Defiance, Maj. William T. H. Brooks, had designated a large pasture on reservation land twelve miles south of the post as a grazing ground for his army horses. It was the same pasture where a Navajo named Manuelito had grazed his own horses for years, as had his father and his grandfather. Brooks warned Manuelito to move his horses. He refused, and Brooks ordered the Indian's horses killed—all sixty of them. Manuelito, known to The People as *Hasteen Chil Haadjiin*, Man of Blackweeds, was a headman of widespread respect. The slaughter of his horses was an insult to all who knew him.

Major Brooks was a West Pointer, class of 1842. He graduated forty-sixth in a class of fifty-one. He might have been a wanton horse-killer, but he also was certified by his diploma to be an officer and a gentleman. He brought with him to the army's most remote outpost a Negro slave, Jim.

Two months after the horse-killing incident, a member of Armijo's band wandered onto the post ostensibly to trade some blankets. He waited his chance, and when nobody was looking he let fly an arrow that went through Jim's lung and killed him. The Indian leaped on his pony and got away.

Brooks was furious. He dashed off a dispatch to the adjutant general asking permission to authorize the Utes to conduct raiding forays against the Navajos under the auspices of the U.S. Army. Permission was granted.

Brooks also suggested that the Utes be allowed to use New Mexican volunteers as their "guides," a switch so outlandish it might have been funny had it not been so wretchedly cynical. Again, permission was granted.

Warming to the challenge, the adjutant general ordered Lt. Col. Dixon S. Miles into the field from a nearby post with a force of "not less than 1,000 men" to find and punish the killer of Major Brooks's houseboy.

Miles arrived at Fort Defiance and sent Sandoval with an ultimatum to the Navajos: they had six days to produce the criminal.

On the sixth day, five hundred unsmiling Navajos rode up to the fort. One walked his horse forward and wordlessly dropped at Miles's feet the limp body of a Mexican youth wrapped in a blanket.

Slave for slave. Possession for possession. It was all The

People could do. It was already more than required to right a wrong among themselves. By Navajo doctrine, crime was avenged and harmony restored not by punishing the criminal physically but by depriving him of something of equal worth. The major's slave was killed in retribution for Manuelito's horses. Manuelito's slave, the Mexican, was double retribution. No one could demand more. The mounted Navajos awaited Miles's reply.

The colonel was up to the occasion: "Sufficient time has been given the Navajo tribe . . . to seek, secure and deliver up the murderer of Major Brooks's Negro; to atone for the insult to our flag, and the many outrages committed on our citizens. They have failed to do so; our duty remains to chastise them into obedience to the observances of our land, and after tomorrow morning war is declared against them."

For the honor of the flag, three columns of U.S. Cavalry fanned out across Dinetah hunting Indians, capturing sheep, razing cornfields, and sacking hogans. After a month only ten of the slippery Navajos were dead and six captured, but the soldiers rounded up a total of eleven thousand sheep and eighty-four horses at the expense of only two men killed and a few wounded. The Navajos, dumbfounded as to why the war began in the first place, had had enough. A group went to Fort Defiance to sue for peace. There they met the commander of the Military Department of New Mexico, Col. B. L. E. Bonneville, the latest of the constantly changing American authorities with whom they had to deal.

Bonneville had a new treaty for the Dineh to sign, which they did on Christmas Day, 1858. It lopped off the eastern third of their inviolate reservation, the portion containing all the rich grazing grounds that the New Mexican stockmen had lusted after for years. The Santa Fe editorial writer must have been pleased about that.

The agent at Fort Defiance, successor to the slain Henry Dodge, was infuriated over the Bonneville Treaty. It was an obvious land-grab clothed in a thin veil of legality. Its terms, wrote agent Samuel M. Yost in an official protest, would require the Navajos "to abandon cultivating the soil and stock raising and become pensioners on the government or plunderers."

If grazing sheep on open ranges rather than watching them starve in the desert could be construed as plundering, then the Navajos were plunderers. And they were plundered as well, in the more recognized sense of the word. Navajo sheep and shepherds who were found outside the new reservation became fair game for Anglo ranchers, who did not overlook the opportunity.

The Dineh struck back, feebly, whenever they could. One day a group of Navajos stampeded a herd of horses which a cavalry unit from Fort Defiance was taking to Albuquerque. The next day the soldier in charge located a young Navajo who had nothing to do with the stampede and asked him to deliver a piece of paper to the Fort Defiance commander, Maj. Oliver L. Shepherd. On the paper was a message reporting the loss of the horses. It is said that the ancient Greeks often killed messengers who brought bad news. Major Shepherd was more compassionate; he had the messenger flogged. On another occasion Major Shepherd shot at a Navajo for not paying attention.

Each atrocity, like the reckless twist of a violin peg, stretched The People's forbearance tighter and tighter.

Sixteen months after the Bonneville Treaty, the string finally broke. At first light on the morning of April 30, 1860, a thousand Navajos stormed the gunports of Fort Defiance screaming out their pent-up anger and firing their arrows. The attack was every bit as valiant as that of Tennyson's Light Brigade, and every bit as futile. Cannon and musket-shot riddled the painted ranks at point-blank range. By sunup, shattered and sundered, the dazed warriors limped back to their hogans.

Naturally the honor of the flag had to be avenged. The inevitable punitive expedition followed, with the same forlorn result as the six that had preceded it. Once again hollow-eyed Navajos trudged wearily past their razed cornfields to the appointed place and signed the usual pledge to mend their barbarous ways.

This time the appointed place was a new army post, Fort Fauntleroy. It was built at Ojo del Oso, that pleasant green valley where fifteen years earlier the suppliant soldier Captain Reid had met the stately Navajo old Narbona. The wheel had turned full circle.

From left to right are the Navajo chiefs Ganada Mucho,
Tiene-su-se, and Mariana (The Smithsonian Institution)

Juanita, the wife of Manuelito
(The Smithsonian Institution)

*Manuelito, a Navajo chief, and his wife were members of a
delegation to Washington in 1874 (The Smithsonian Institution)*

Above: Chee Dodge, an Indian trader
(Museum of New Mexico)

Left: Manuelito Segundo, the son of
Manuelito and Juanita
(The Smithsonian Institution)

Left: Rations are issued to a oup of Navajo Indians, c. 1879

Right: An old Navajo warrior ith lance and shield, c. 1892
(both photos from The
Smithsonian Institution)

*Soil erosion has damaged thousands of
acres of Navajo land and firewood is scarce
(Culver Pictures, Inc., above;
Paul Conklin, below)*

Sheep, brought into Navajo territory in the sixteenth century by the Spaniards, remain an important source of food and income (Culver Pictures, Inc., left; Paul Conklin, right)

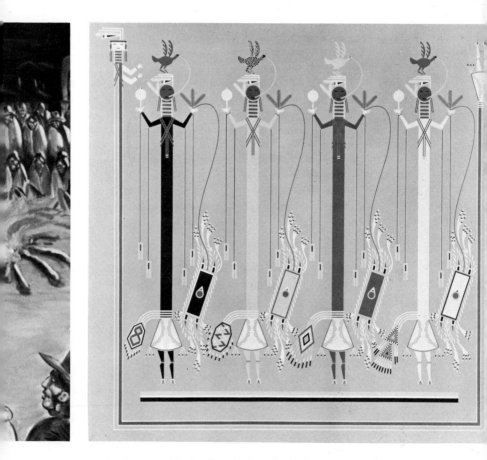

*Left: A naturalistic oil painting depicting
a Yeibichai dance (Paul Conklin)*

*Above: A traditional Navajo sand painting
(Museum of New Mexico)*

Right: Two Navajo men meticulously create a sand painting (Museum of New Mexico—Santa Fe Railway Photograph)

Below: A completed buffalo sand painting (New Mexico State Tourist Bureau)

*Navajo women perfected
the art of rug weaving
centuries ago and use
virtually the same
techniques now as then
(New Mexico Department
of Development)*

*Above: A Navajo woman and her daughter
make baking mats of cornhusks
(Museum of New Mexico)*

*Right: A group of Navajo women attend
classes to learn the dying art of basket making
(Paul Conklin)*

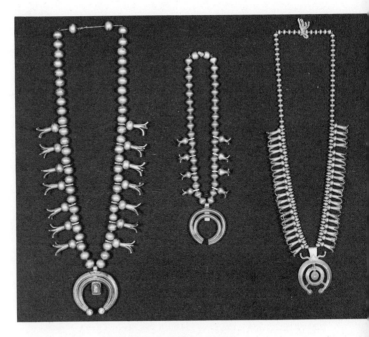

*Navajo silversmiths are noted for their
exquisite jewelry (Museum of New Mexico, left;
New Mexico State Tourist Bureau, above)*

Much of the Navajos' land is harsh but majestically beautiful (Paul Conklin)

Below, a traditional hogan made of dried mud and sticks; at right, the interior of a modern hogan made of wood and plaster (Paul Conklin)

*At left, children learn to read in Navajo
on the reservation; below, Navajo women
attend a driver training class at Navajo
Community College (Paul Conklin)*

Reservation schools offer classes for all ages. The woman at left is learning to read English. The students below attend Navajo Community College (Paul Conklin)

Above: These Navajo school children are being checked by a team of Public Health Service eye doctors

Left: Federal funds provide some Navajos with training for construction work (both photos by Paul Conklin)

A voter casts his ballot for tribal chairman (Paul Conklin)

PLAN OF BATTLE

"THE MEN ARE TO BE SLAIN"

CHAPTER ELEVEN

The day was April 25, 1861. In the broad meadow of Tsehotsohih, the soldiers were striking camp, abandoning Fort Defiance. The news spread, and The People gathered in wordless clusters on the red sandstone ridges to watch. Navajo runners arrived with breathtaking reports that the same thing was happening at Fort Fauntleroy, at Abiquiu, and at army posts up and down the Rio Grande. Soldiers throughout the territory were bidding one another forced farewells and marching eastward. There was excited talk about a fort unknown to The People, Fort Sumter. The whole strange business was something a benighted Indian could not be expected to understand.

With the bluecoats gone off to fight among themselves, The People once again became Lords of the Earth. Even the First New Mexican Volunteers, organized into a Union regiment under Col. Christopher ("Kit") Carson, was too busy repelling a Confederate attack up the Rio Grande to bother about Indians. Navajo and Apache raids on the frontier ranches and Indian pueblos were never more frequent nor more proficient. The People replenished their flocks, planted their valleys, visited their sacred mountains, and slept in their hogans without fear for the first time in years.

The freewheeling days were destined to be brief, however, for both the Navajos and for the small tribe of Mescalero Apaches.

In Santa Fe at the time, sent there from California with a Union regiment to reinforce Colonel Carson's ragtag horde, was a man whose name would live as a curse on Navajo lips. He was Brig. Gen. James Henry Carleton, a professional soldier with dark eyes, an uncontrollable mop of dark hair, a droopy mustache, cheek whiskers, and an abiding dislike of Indians.

Indians, Carleton believed, "can no more be trusted than the wolves that run through the mountains." With equal callousness but some perception he once said that the Navajo in particular was "a more watchful and a more wary animal than a deer; he must be hunted with skill."

By the fall of 1862 the Confederate threat to New Mexico had been thoroughly crushed. Carleton and Carson, with two regiments of soldiers at hand and no rebels to fight, got approval from Washington to heed the pleas of the New Mexicans and turn their troops against the marauding Indians.

According to New Mexico's Gov. Henry Connelly, the Navajos were keeping "an immense pastoral and mining population," his constituents, from properly developing all that rich New Mexico land. "The public interest," he told his territorial legislature, "demands that this condition of things should cease to exist. Too long have they roamed Lords of the Soil over this extensive and valuable tract of country. They are entitled to a portion of it for their maintenance but to no more."

The portion General Carleton picked for the Navajos' maintenance was the *Llano Estacado*, the Staked Plains, one of the most desolate expanses of desert on the continent.

The Pecos River rises in the mountains near Santa Fe, takes a southeasterly course, and when it reaches the Staked Plains cuts a thin ribbon of life through that abominable wasteland. At a point roughly 160 miles due west of Albuquerque, the river arcs around a grove of cottonwood trees 16 miles long and ½ mile wide, the only green vegetation for miles. The Mexicans called the spot *Bosque Redondo*, Round Grove.

At Bosque Redondo, General Carleton established a small adobe army post and named it Fort Sumner. It was to be the place of exile for the Navajos and the Mescalero Apaches. Never mind that the Navajos by treaty, or rather treaties, already had a reservation. Fort Sumner, at the Bosque Redondo, would be their Egypt.

Carleton minced no words about his intent. "Among all my endeavors since my arrival here," he reported to his superior, "has been an effort to brush back the Indians . . . so that the people [white Americans] could get out of the valley of the Rio Grande and not only possess themselves of the arable lands in other parts of the territory but, if the country contained veins and deposits of precious metals, that they might be found." In other words, rid the woods of "those pernicious creatures, to make room for a better growth."

The Mescaleros were first. Their domain was south of the Navajos', and they were equally despised by the settlers in those parts. They were also equally elusive when pursued. The bounty in Silver City for an Apache scalp was $250. Carleton's orders to Kit Carson were direct and uncomplicated: "The men are to be slain whenever and wherever they can be found. The women and children may be taken prisoners. . . ." By March of 1863 Carson had rounded up about 350 Mescaleros, all he could catch, and had sent them to the Fort Sumner concentration camp.

The Navajos were next. General Carleton's preparations were systematic and thorough. First he built a new post, Fort Wingate, about forty miles east of the abandoned camp at Ojo del Oso and garrisoned it with 300 men. It would serve as a way station for the anticipated eastward migration of the Indians. Next he reactivated Fort Defiance. It would serve as operational headquarters for his field commander, Colonel Carson. Finally he stationed detachments of his own regiment along all the familiar Navajo raiding routes to the Rio Grande—the mountain passes and stream beds—plugging every eastern exit from Navajo country. He wanted there to be no escape. The tactics of the campaign he left entirely in the hands of Col. Christopher Carson.

Kit Carson at fifty-three was already a national legend. Born in Kentucky, he adventured out to Taos, New Mexico, at seventeen and spent the next two decades trapping beaver in the mountain streams of the American West all the way to the Pacific and from border to border, earning the respect and admiration of his fellow Mountain Men. Unlike the hard-drinking, loud-boasting stereotype of his breed, however, Kit Carson was quiet, self-effacing, and laconic. At his ranch near Taos he kept a library of some 150 books.

Carson served as chief scout for John C. Frémont's three surveying expeditions and owed his well-deserved fame as a trail blazer and Indian fighter to Frémont's best-selling accounts of the journeys. Frémont extolled his scout's exploits, thereby luring waves of journalists westward to romanticize them further. Most of Kit Carson's deeds did not need romanticizing. When the Civil War broke out, Taos was a hotbed of Confederate sympathy. On a day when the rebels were particularly restless Kit Carson strode to the town plaza with an American flag, nailed it to a cottonwood staff, stood beneath it with his rifle at the ready, and dared anyone to pull the banner down. None dared. To this day the flag in Taos plaza is one of the few permitted by Congress to fly night and day.

Colonel Carson's First New Mexico Volunteers were a regiment of 400 undisciplined New Mexicans who rarely wore army uniforms, rarely received army pay, rarely had enough horses to go around, and rarely all showed up when it was time to do battle. Carson decided that they would not be sufficient for the job he planned to do.

The call went out for more volunteers. As in the past, many New Mexicans took it as an invitation for legalized plunder and slave raids. So frantically did they rush to offer their services that the governor had to call off the stampede by official proclamation.

Kit Carson, even though his first wife was a Cheyenne,

had no scruples about enslaving Indians (which is more a comment on how the practice was regarded in the territory generally than on Carson's own sense of ethics). The Emancipation Proclamation meant as little to most New Mexicans as it did to most southern planters; it would be a safe guess that there were more slaves per capita in New Mexico than in any Confederate state, where only the very wealthy could afford them. (The comparison is not wholly sound. Unlike the Negro, the Indian was not considered a slave from birth by accident of race.) Carson pressed into service scores of Pueblo and Ute warriors to help conquer the Navajos and asked specifically that the Utes be allowed to keep their captives. Carson had served as agent for the Utes and knew well the one, sure incentive that would lure them to battle. Besides, he told General Carleton, the more Navajos enslaved, the fewer the government would have to feed later. What's more, he argued, "their being distributed as servants through the territory causes them to lose that collectiveness of interest as a tribe which they will retain if kept together."

Carleton turned down Carson's request. Making slaves of people would hardly be a fit policy for a government currently warring to free them. The best he would allow Carson's mercenaries, officially, was a bounty of twenty dollars for every captured horse or mule and one dollar for each sheep. Unofficially, the general's *pro forma* denial was thoroughly ignored. Navajo lore abounds with stories of enslavement, and written accounts confirm them. Indian trader Nathan Bibo, for example, wrote of the volunteer unit recruited by Ramón A. Baca of Cebolleta: "They took hundreds of prisoners, who, as was the custom . . . were sold as domestics all over the territory."

On June 19, 1863, Kit Carson was equipped and ready. He rode at the head of a column of 736 officers and men, a train of supply wagons, and teams of mules dragging four mountain-howitzers. A fife-and-drum corps led the parade through the dusty streets of Taos beneath the flag still boldly flying. The colonel's lady sat in her carriage at the western edge of town to wave farewell with a moist handkerchief, and the men in the ranks had a brave song for the occasion:

> *Come dress your ranks, my gallant souls,*
> *A-standing in a row,*
> *Kit Carson he is waiting*
> *To march against the foe;*
> *At night we march to Moqui*
> *O'er lofty hills of snow,*
> *To meet and crush the savage foe:*
> *Bold Johnny Navajo.*
> *Johnny Navajo!*
> *O Johnny Navajo!*

But it was not to be that kind of a war. There would be no flashing sabers and singing bugles, no thundering waves of bluecoats dashing to the fray. It was to be the only kind of war which could bring the Navajos to their "brutal senses," in General Carleton's revealing phrase, the only kind of war for which the men of Kit Carson's command were suited: a maximum of looting and destruction, a minimum of discipline, and no fighting. The American army did not intend to meet the enemy in combat. Bold Johnny Navajo would simply be starved to death.

THE LONG WALK

CHAPTER TWELVE

Beasos Dihi, Dark Feather, of the clan of Coyote Pass People, lived near Canyon de Chelly and was much admired by all whose hogans were in the vicinity. His people also called him *Hasteen Daghaa*, Whiskered Man. A rather forlorn mustache framed his mouth. The Spanish had given him the name *Barboncito*, Little Whiskers, and that was the name the Americans called him as well. His own people had yet another name for Barboncito. They called him *Hozhoonzhi Naataanii*, Leader of Peace. He was a singer who could perform the Blessing Way ceremony, the holiest of all Navajo rites, and his very voice soothed his listeners with its solemnity and calmness. Indeed, the Navajos called him *bizahalani*, a special word to describe a "man of eloquence."

From the beginning Barboncito had sought the path of peace with the Americans. He had put his X to the original treaty, the Doniphan Treaty of 1846, and was one of the headmen who pleaded with Colonel Bonneville for an end to the murderous campaign of 1858. But even this man of peace had a limit to the insults he could endure. The Bonneville Treaty was not what he had been led to believe would be offered and he did not sign it. Later, during the night-long discussions among the headmen which ended in the glorious but futile assault on Fort Defiance, Barboncito, along with his militant friend Manuelito and a bold companion named Herrero, had counseled in favor of the attack. Others had argued against the venture but Barboncito's eloquence and acknowledged wisdom won out. The defeat in no way diminished his standing among his people.

The young men of the tribe came frequently to Barboncito during the winter of 1862 with reports of renewed activity at long-deserted Fort Defiance and with news of the new fort, Fort Wingate, being built to the southeast. They also had heard that the Americans were driving the Apaches deeper into the mountains to the south.

Alarmed, Barboncito and his brother *Delgadito*, Thin Man, along with sixteen other Navajos, journeyed to Santa Fe to talk to the new American leader, General Carleton. If he merely wanted them to make their Xs on a piece of paper, they would be glad to oblige Carleton now, and there would be no need for the usual killing and burning. Carleton dismissed them with a wave of the hand.

Six months later, on June 23, 1863, while Kit Carson and his troops were making their way toward Dinetah, Barboncito got his reply.

A messenger arrived from Fort Wingate with General Carleton's ultimatum. The Navajos had until July 20 to surrender themselves unconditionally to the soldiers at Fort Defiance and to be led to a new place of residence far beyond the Rio Grande. After that date "every Navajo that is seen will be considered as hostile and treated accordingly." That meant killed or captured.

The deadline passed and none surrendered. Kit Carson moved out with his troops. He pitched his camps at places convenient to The People's most fertile croplands and pastures and ranged out day by day in all directions. His men systematically destroyed every food plant and burned every hogan they could find. When the large fields were gone, they sought out the smaller ones, then the smaller ones still.

They did not bother chasing Indians. If small bands came threateningly close, cannoneers kept them at bay with howitzers while foot soldiers worked with machetes and torches.

Carson saw that his men overlooked nothing. Crops capable of growing back without replanting were carefully pulled up by the roots. Fruit trees were hacked down at ground level. Caches of wheat and shelled corn—"as fine as the territory produced," wrote Carson—were burned after the troops had taken their fill. Sheep, too numerous to butcher and too burdensome to return for bounty, were slaughtered by the tens upon tens of thousands in orgies of marksmanship and their carcasses left to rot on the hillsides.

Carson estimated that he had laid waste two million pounds of foodstuffs and an untold number of animals before the month was over. Deeper and deeper into Dinetah he pushed his army, a human scythe sparing nothing in its path and leaving behind only stubble and embers and acres of stinking flesh. Through river valleys and canyons Kit Carson's hordes swept, pillaging and plundering.

The People fled in bewildered terror before the unholy onslaught. Some went south and west to search out the hideaways of the surviving Mescaleros. Others went north and west to the sacred fastness of Navajo Mountain. Some went to Grand Canyon, others to the wild ravines along the Little Colorado, still others to the unexplored basin of the lower San Juan.

But mostly they went where down through the centuries they had always gone when trouble threatened. They went to the forbidding cliffs and secret niches of an unfailing bastion of security, Canyon de Chelly, to hide until the current danger passed. Only this danger was different from any The People had ever faced in all their long history. This danger would not pass, because when the soldiers were gone the ruin would remain, and there would be nothing for The People to eat. Nothing.

Kit Carson led his troops back to Fort Defiance, put away his horse, and waited for winter. "I can take no pride in this fearful destruction," Carson wrote to his wife. "My sleep is haunted by dreams of starving Navajo squaws and children. If the elders of the tribe would listen to reason, we could make peace. But they're stubborn men, so I must finish what I have started."

Listen to reason? By Navajo reason life was not sustained merely by the lungs breathing air and the heart pumping blood. A Navajo's pulse throbbed with the rhythm of his world, beat for beat. His world was Dinetah. Beyond the embrace of his sacred mountains there could be no rhythm for him, no harmony, no life. Listen to reason? On October 21 a delegation of Navajos trudged to Fort Defiance to plead for reason. They were told they could either leave their land or remain and starve. To The People the choice was spiritual death or physical death. By what reasoning could a Navajo choose? Death is death.

The autumn leaves blew. Still The People refused to go into Fort Defiance to deliver themselves to the soldiers. They scavenged the woods and the high ridges for piñon nuts and cedar berries and implored their gods for deliverance, but they did not go in. Soon the snow swirled. They gathered yucca fruit in the lowlands and grubbed in the frozen earth for wild potatoes, but they did not go in. December yielded to January. Many froze to death, and many starved to death, but they did not go in.

Kit Carson saw only one course open to him. On January 6, 1864, he led his troops to Canyon de Chelly.

It took eleven days to complete the mission. Carson divided his men into three groups and sent them on separate paths of destruction through the three main branches of the Y-shaped gorge. At their approach, The People crawled into ever deeper recesses. They even took refuge in the ancient cliffside homes of the Anasazi, uttering prayers and covering themselves with ashes before entering to ward off the *chindi*, the "evil spirit" who hovers about the dwellings of the dead.

Some shouted curses at the pillaging troops, a last, pitiful gesture of defiance. The soldiers showed no mercy to the Indians. One of the Navajos who fell to their bullets was Barboncito's brother, *El Sordo*, Deaf Man. Others who were killed, according to one of Carson's lieutenants, included two men and a woman who "obstinately persisted in hurling rocks and pieces of wood." Most, however, were too weak to fight back.

For the most part The People could only huddle in woebegone silence in their miserable niches. They dared not light fires to keep warm; the glow might betray them by night, the smoke by day. They dared not even stir to hunt piñon nuts. When darkness fell, a few stole down to the peach orchards below to gather the unharvested fruit, dragging clumps of brush behind them to erase their moccasin tracks in the snow. Soon even the rotten, frozen peaches were denied them. The soldiers cut down 3,000 trees before they quit counting. They left not one.

Kit Carson knew then that it would only be a matter of time. The People would come into Fort Defiance. He was not wrong.

They straggled to the fort in small groups, gaunt, weak, and weary. By February more than 800 had arrived. Within thirty days their numbers tripled. They found no shelter at the bleak outpost save their own blankets, and the food the soldiers issued was stuff they had not seen before. They were given coffee beans. The women boiled them as they would pinto beans, each time pouring off the dark water. The beans never became edible. Neither did the flour. The women tried boiling it, tried mixing it into a gruel. It only made them choke. Dysentery took over. At least 126 Navajos doubled up in agony and died.

On March 6, 1864, the soldiers prodded the Navajos to their feet and formed them into a long line. Thirty supply wagons pulled out in front; the aged and the lame climbed aboard them where there was room. The animals brought up the rear, 473 horses and 3,000 sheep. A soldier growled the command to move out. The 2,400 emaciated refugees turned numbly to face the morning sun. The Long Walk began.

A week later another group left. A week after that another, then another until more than 8,500 souls stretched in mournful procession across the great Southwest.

The 350-mile journey took more than three weeks. It followed the worn military road to Fort Wingate and on past the awesome lava flow which The People knew to be the dried blood of the monster *Yeitso* slain by the Hero Twin. It wound around the base of mist-shrouded *Tsodzil* —Mount Taylor, the limit of Dinetah. Beyond that holy peak lay an alien land, a land not ordained for The People, a land of sorrow where they knew they could find no peace.

Each day some of the travelers died, and the path became a trail of corpses. Some too sick to go on were shot. The weary column forded the Rio Grande at Isleta Pueblo. It was a treacherous crossing during the spring flood, and at times the old and the feeble gave up in midstream, and at times the roily, yellow waters washed infants from their mothers' weakened arms. The soldier escorts had their own sickening sport; when Navajo women died they cut off their breasts and tossed them about like baseballs.

Thirteen miles north of Isleta, at Los Pinos near present day Albuquerque, The People were herded for the night into a large corral, a pen with two bells hanging from its entrance gate. There, slave raiders lay in wait and preyed on each group that passed, carrying off women to the nearby city. Since that time, Albuquerque has been known in the language of The People as The Place of the Bells.

Beyond Albuquerque stretched only the plain, a wasteland of scrub cactus and greasewood, a land without shadows. And beyond the plain, the Bosque Redondo and Fort Sumner.

The fort was a collection of adobe buildings cooked to a dreary brown by the merciless sun. The buildings were set on flat, brown earth, forming a compound: seven squat, brown buildings for officers, six for enlisted men; a squat, brown hospital; a squat, brown bakehouse; a squat, brown guardhouse; four squat, brown storehouses; and three squat, brown stables. Nearby, the brown waters of the Pecos stank of alkali. At the fort's approaches soldiers stood wearily with guns.

The People called Fort Sumner *Hwelte*. It was the closest their tongue could approximate to the Spanish word the soldiers used, *Fuerte*, The Strong Place—the end of The Long Walk.

HWELTE

CHAPTER THIRTEEN

The People filed into the fenced compound at Hwelte. They sank to the bare ground in forlorn family clusters. There was no shelter. The night wind off the Staked Plain chilled their naked bodies. Thin arms cradled listless infants and wrapped them in pitiful shreds of blankets. Bony fingers wrestled tough mesquite knots from the desert floor and coaxed them into reluctant fires. The People did not weep before their captors or cry out or grovel. They had not the strength. Across the compound they turned hollow eyes heavenward and pleaded only to the stars for surcease of their sorrow in the sweet oblivion of sleep.

If Brig. Gen. James H. Carleton, the architect of their misery, interpreted the Navajos' apparent resignation as humble acceptance of their prison home, he could not have been more wrong. The gods who shaped The People as Beings Created From Everything placed within every Navajo soul a burning sense of personal liberty, and within the collective tribal soul an abiding notion of cultural independence that no amount of privation could extinguish. The soldiers of the nineteenth century and the bureaucrats of the twentieth would never be convinced of that, but it was so. An eloquent Navajo presented to history only as an unnamed witness in a government document tried patiently to explain the fundamental mystery of his people to an official at Fort Sumner:

> *There is something within us which does not speak but thinks, and though we remain silent our faces speak to one another.*
> *Cage the badger and he will try to break from his prison and regain his native hole. Chain the eagle to the ground—he will strive to gain his freedom, and though he fails, he will lift his head and look up to the sky which is his home. And we want to return to our mountains and our meadows.*

General Carleton had other ideas. Having presided over the most wanton campaign of destruction in American military history, an operation that made Sherman's march through Georgia the following year seem humane by comparison, Carleton was now gripped with all the tender zeal of a misguided missionary.

All he wanted to do, he told his adjutant general, was to collect the Navajos together "little by little, on a reservation, away from their haunts and hills and hiding places of their country, and then . . . to be kind to them, teach their children how to read and write, teach them the arts of peace . . . the truths of Christianity. Soon they would acquire new habits, new ideas, new modes of life . . . [and] become a happy and contented people."

He overlooked one thing. Happy and contented people have to eat. For all the diabolical thoroughness of his military campaign, the object of which was to starve the Navajos into submission, Carleton neglected to make any plans to feed his eighty-five hundred potential catechumens anything other than the leftovers from his own army kitchens.

It was a problem he would have to solve himself; he would get no help from the Indian Bureau. It was true that for fifteen years administration of Indian affairs had been a function of the Interior Department, but Michael Steck, the department's New Mexico superintendent, viewed the Navajo matter as strictly a military concern. The army had conceived of the Navajo roundup during a period of martial law in the territory, had carried it out, had financed it, and now was stuck with it. Steck's budget, he quibbled, did not include anything for Navajo upkeep.

It was typically American bureaucratic infighting and sadly reminiscent of a dispute two generations earlier at the highest levels of government. That quarrel ended in the criminal eradication of the Cherokee Nation, the largest of the Iroquoian tribes and culturally one of the most advanced.

The Cherokees occupied the mountainous juncture of Georgia, North Carolina, and Tennessee. They had long since evolved an alphabet and had a written constitution. Their government included executive, legislative, and judicial branches, an Iroquoian development which predated America's colonization. In 1794 the Cherokee and United States governments agreed by treaty to national boundaries.

In 1828 gold was discovered in Georgia. As was inevitable, the state legislature confiscated all the Cherokee land and parceled it out to white Georgians by lottery. The Cherokees appealed to the United States Supreme Court.

Chief Justice John Marshall handed down a decision in 1832. It declared that the Cherokee Nation was "a distinct community . . . in which the laws of Georgia can have no force and which the citizens of Georgia have no right to enter but with the assent of the Cherokees themselves." Snorted President Andrew Jackson: "John Marshall has rendered his decision, now let him enforce it." The Cherokees were driven out of Georgia, and the United States Army herded them along the Trail of Tears to Oklahoma. There they perished as a nation, and their rich culture crumbled.

In New Mexico in 1864 the Navajos were the pawns in the bureaucratic squabble, and Michael Steck was saying in effect: James Carleton has made his mess, now let him clean it up.

That was all right with Carleton. He was consummately jealous concerning his mad scheme and like a man possessed was determined to see it through. He put his own men on half rations and also consigned to the Navajos food the army condemned as unfit, much of it crawling with vermin and contaminated with rat droppings. "The Indians are to be fed at the rate of *one* pound for each man, woman and child per day, of fresh meat, or of corn, or of wheat, or of wheat meal, or of corn meal, or of flour, or of kraut, or of pickles. . . . Or in lieu of any one of these articles, half a pound of beans, or of rice, or of peas, or of dried fruit."

Carleton was convinced that the starvation diet would be temporary. He had his captives out in the fields every day, twelve hours a day, digging irrigation ditches, grubbing out the gnarled mesquite with their hands—they had no tools—and planting fifteen hundred acres of corn. Meanwhile dysentery took its agonizing toll, and infants died daily of malnutrition.

The prisoners still slept on the open ground or in gravelike dugouts of their own design roofed over with brush. But that condition could be endured temporarily too, Carleton felt, for his vision was little short of paradise: "By having a judicious site selected and the spare time of the families spent in putting up their houses, by next winter they can all be comfortably sheltered. Then to have trees planted to make shade, and I fancy there would be no Indian village in the world to compare with it in point of beauty."

Carleton envisaged some sort of Navajo pueblo. When The People learned of it they said they would refuse to dwell in such a place. Where would their old ones go to die? They explained about the chindi and the necessity of burning a hogan where death had occurred. They explained that that was why they refused to go to the army hospital, a place of death. One of them told the post surgeon, George Gwyther, that they wanted no part of him or his medicine: "We are afraid of it. We prefer our own singers. They don't kill if they cannot cure."

Desperate to devise a plan for housing such superstitious creatures, Carleton sent for Kit Carson, the Indian expert. Carson said why not let them live in hogans? Carleton said very well, but the hogans would have to be in uniform rows like a proper city. If anyone felt he had to burn a hogan, he could rebuild at the end of the row. Carleton visualized ten separate villages, with happy little Navajos frolicking in the streets.

In late summer of 1864 the corn crop failed. Carleton blamed the cutworm. The People knew better. It was not ordained that Navajos should live at the Bosque Redondo. To them the land was cursed.

Carleton's persistent appeals to Washington for food and clothing became frantic. "The Indians are quite naked," he wrote. At length Congress appropriated $100,-000 for supplies. With customary bureaucratic efficiency, the goods were purchased in the East. When the wagons arrived at Fort Sumner—ironically, at Christmas time—they contained scarcely $30,000 worth of supplies at local prices. General Carleton wrung his hands. He also ordered that the skins of butchered animals be distributed for moccasins.

In Santa Fe, citizens began to grumble about Carleton's experiment. Before long the criticism swelled into a territorial chorus. Newspapers trumpeted every new failure at the Bosque Redondo and with bitter sarcasm nicknamed the Navajo reservation "Fair Carletonia." The general bristled. "Every intelligent man in the country approves it," he whined to a distant superior.

It would be gratifying to believe that New Mexico's citizens were humanely concerned about naked, starving Indians, and perhaps some were, but the *Santa Fe New Mexican* provided another reason. Carleton, an editorial said, had made "one of our most fertile valleys an asylum for the Indians of another territory; removing them from 300 to 400 miles east against the current of emigration and improvement."

Indians were meant to be pushed westward to starve, not eastward; Carleton had moved them the wrong direction. Now they were described as Indians of another territory—Arizona, formed in 1863, and New Mexicans wanted no part of them. Kit Carson was even more candid in a deposition to Congress: "Some [New] Mexicans," he said, "now object to the settlement of the Navajos at the Bosque because they can't prey on them as formerly."

When spring came Carleton sent his prisoners back into the fields. They doubled the previous year's fifteen hundred acres, planted a crop of wheat to supplement the corn, and dug more irrigation ditches.

Food became so scarce in that "most fertile valley" that Carleton had to issue ration tickets—slips of cardboard. The Navajos quickly learned to make counterfeit ones. Carleton withdrew the cardboard tickets and substituted metal disks. Skilled silversmiths, the Navajos duplicated the metal disks. Exasperated, Carleton sent to Washington for printed tickets of intricate design. Those the Navajos could not duplicate.

The 1865 crop failed.

The second winter at Hwelte was more severe than the first. The thin woods nearby were stripped bare, and The People had to travel twenty miles to cut logs for their fires. They suffered through. When the ground thawed, Carleton doggedly ordered the cultivated ground tripled in area, nine thousand acres, and he had them plant five thousand trees for future fuel.

The People knew it was useless. The land along the Pecos was not their land; it would not provide for them. A special agent of the Interior Department arrived from Washington to investigate. Barboncito's friend, Herrero, tried to explain to the agent that the people enjoyed harmony with all of the creations of nature, but only in their own land, Dinetah: "We think that in the world, on the earth, and in the heavens we are all equal and we have all been born by the same mother. What we want is to be sent back to our own land. Even if we starve there we will have no complaints to make.

"As poor as we are we would rather go back to our land. What does the government want us to do? More than we have done? More than we are doing?"

The days of privation and exile passed, each day more sorrowful than the last. The longing for beloved Dinetah became too much for some of The People to endure. When warm weather came it was time to act.

Each night in the darkness, a few at a time, family by family, group by group, The People began to leave the accursed Bosque Redondo. Without sound they slipped out of their rude brush shelters, crept past Carleton's pickets, forded the stinking Pecos, and vanished in the moonlight. Without food or water they headed west in the silence of the night, following a star and drawn by an inexorable urge. We know from Navajo lore that some survived hunger, thirst, and the unyielding desert and made it home. We know also that many did not.

General Carleton was outraged. At first he refused, ostrichlike, even to admit that Navajos were fleeing Fair

Carletonia in droves. But his own counting system soon made the fact undeniable; by June more than a thousand Indians were not turning in daily ration tickets for their allotted scraps. In a screaming fit Carleton fired off a communiqué to his post commander: "Tell the Indians I will cause to be killed every Indian I find off the reservation without a passport. A great many have been killed in the Navajo country. The troops are now fast coming in from the plains, and we will be sure to catch them. Tell them this!"

In rapid order the whole structure of General Carleton's great experiment began to fall apart. The Indian superintendent, Michael Steck, resigned. His successor was relieved, and a third man took over. The post commander at Fort Sumner was relieved and another appointed. The post quartermaster was court-martialed for selling army beef. The Indian agent was fired for buying it. The New Mexico legislature clamored for Carleton's dismissal. Unprecedented hailstorms ravaged the post. Bands of Comanches raided its livestock.

The 1866 crop failed.

On September 19, 1866, Brig. Gen. James Henry Carleton was relieved of command of the Military District of New Mexico.

Winter descended upon the exiles of Hwelte for the third time. Around their campfires they discussed their lot and in whispers plotted a mass escape for the following summer. They would return to Dinetah or die in the attempt.

In the spring they refused to plant yet another crop of corn. The soldiers insisted, forcing them to the fields at bayonet point. Emboldened by their own escape plans and dreams of Dinetah, The People struck back when the opportunity arose. By summer they had ambushed and killed five soldiers. They watched the foul Pecos dry up to a trickle under a blistering sun. The disfavor of the gods was clear.

But now their headmen advised The People against escape. More inspectors had arrived at Hwelte. Their future, The People were told, was no longer in the hands of the military. The Department of the Interior was at last putting civilians in charge of Indian affairs. That was what the Navajos were told. Patience, the headmen counseled, was the wiser course.

The 1867 crop, of course, failed.

THE TREATY OF 1868

"DO AS BARBONCITO TELLS YOU"

CHAPTER FOURTEEN

The Department of the Interior was, on paper at least, the agency of the government responsible for dealing with Indians. But for many years its Indian Bureau was staffed by soldiers, and the Navajos were naive to believe that the civilian agents would have much voice in deciding The People's future. Telling the Indians that the agents could help them might have been a nice ploy to discourage the restless Navajos in their mass escape plans, but it was hardly true.

The petulant Michael Steck, the Indian affairs superintendent in Santa Fe who was annoyed with his budget and had been more than willing to wash his hands of the whole Fort Sumner mess and let the military stew in its own juice, had reported to Washington in 1865 that it was his "firm conviction that more can be accomplished upon a suitable reservation in their own country with an appropriation of $250,000 than at the Pecos with $2 million." He had pointed out that the Bosque Redondo was "almost destitute of wood, [had] a scanty supply of water, no building timber and no shelter for stock against the storms of winter." But when all these predictions of failure proved true, Agent Steck still refused to come forth and assert himself, even if only to gloat. Instead, he resigned.

Whatever the reason for his silence, the following year Washington sent a special agent, J. K. Graves, to Fort Sumner to recommend the proper way to dispose of the Navajos. Steck, the eternal bureaucrat, had no stomach for bucking rank. Graves, his superior, became an overnight expert on the Navajos and found every reason to leave them right where they were, at Fort Sumner. His main argument had a familiar ring and had nothing to do with the welfare of the Navajos.

"The location of the Navajos upon this [Fort Sumner] reservation as their government home," he reported, "will leave open for future settlement the vast section now known as the Navajo Country which, being of a mountainous nature and known to contain rich mineral wealth . . ." and so forth, a reasoning process harking back to the viceroys of Spain.

Besides, Graves went on, the Navajos themselves had told him that if they had to live outside their own country they might just as well stay at the Bosque Redondo. In the manner of men everywhere with their minds made up, Graves could interpret "as bad a place as any" to mean "as good a place as any." "However," he felt compelled to add, "they claim that here as elsewhere outside of their old homes they will dwindle and soon fade away. It will require time and patience to wholly remove this superstitious belief from their minds."

The balance of Special Agent Graves's report offers a revealing glimpse of the official view of history accepted by the white Easterner of the 1860s. He continued:

> *Like all Indians the Navajos prefer their own country and it is quite natural they should. Yet in view of the past experience of the Government with, and the well known history of, this Tribe, they should never again be permitted to occupy their former homes.*
>
> *For centuries this Tribe roamed the country, the terror to all the people. When pursued in retaliation for their atrocious deeds they fled to their mountain fastnesses, and, secreting themselves in their numerous retreats and ravines, wholly inaccessible to civilized man, calmly awaited a fitting opportunity to emerge again upon their wicked path of action. Or if perchance any were captured, they invariably implored for peace, and as being the shortest method and surest road to an immediate cessation of Indian depredations, the military authorities invariably extended the olive branch—released the captives, who, instead of returning to their people and imploring them to recognize the solemn stipulations connected with their release, disregarded alike their work and their magnanimous captors who had spared their lives—united themselves to their brethren and with the swoop of the eagle dashed down the mountain sides and renewed their revolting series of murder and pillage.*
>
> *Return to their former homes the Navajos now located at the Bosque Redondo reservation and war will speedily ensue. . . .*

By 1868, however, it had become a matter not of tactics or humanitarianism but of simple economics. After four successive crop failures at Fort Sumner, the fact that the area's alkaline soil would never grow corn was obvious even to a myopic bureaucrat. The Navajos' magnanimous captors, despite Agent Graves's logic, were simply going to have to move The People elsewhere. The Indian wars were costing the American people $1,000,000 for every Indian killed; keeping them in a concentration camp was hardly less expensive. In one seven-month period at Fort Sumner it cost $452,356.98 just to provide the captives with their meager starvation rations. The alternatives, as the Interior Department saw them, were either to move the Navajos to some more productive place or to feed them forever.

The department's struggle to wrest control of Indian affairs from the military required many years and miles of red tape because of the military's characteristic reluctance to let go of anything. As always, the soldiers didn't like civilians chipping away at their prerogatives, even if it was the law. Thus, orders issued in Washington were mysteriously lost, ignored, or sidetracked en route to New Mexico. Meanwhile, the Navajos endured their fourth winter at Hwelte.

Even after civilians finally gained the upper hand, nearly a year elapsed before the newly organized Peace Commission could turn its attention from the time-consuming business of exterminating the Plains tribes and deal with the already subjugated Navajos.

Finally, in mid-May of 1868, Gen. William Tecumseh Sherman and Sen. Samuel F. Tappan, members of the commission, arrived at Fort Sumner to "negotiate a treaty" with the Navajos, which meant that they would tell the Indians where they would have to live.

On May 28, Sherman and Tappan called a council with the Navajo headmen to allow them to present their case. Translation, as always, was a problem. After twenty-two years of administering the affairs of the New Mexico Territory, there still was not a single white man available who could speak Navajo. Kit Carson could manage a few words, but Carson (to the sorrow of General Sherman, who greatly admired him) had died the previous week from injuries received in a fall from a horse. There was one man among the captives, Jesus Arviso, who could speak Spanish as well as Navajo. Arviso was a Mexican by birth. The Apaches had captured him as a boy in Sonora around 1850 and had traded him for a horse to a Navajo named Black Shirt. Arviso grew up as a Navajo, and The People accepted him as one of their own. He could take the place of the renegade Sandoval, who had dropped out of history in the early 1860s. (The People have several theories as to what became of Sandoval, none of them pleasant.) General Sherman sent for Arviso and for a Spanish-English translator, James Sutherland. These negotiations, like all the others, would be carried out by using the clumsy method of translation and retranslation.

The first choice of The People for their spokesman at the council was the much admired Barboncito, the *bizahalani*, the "man of eloquence." Barboncito had made The Long Walk to Fort Sumner with his people, but almost as soon as he arrived, he and his close friend Manuelito escaped. They made their way back home and held out two years longer before they were recaptured. Since then, Barboncito was among the headmen who had counseled against escape, sensing that change was in the offing. Other men of stature went with Barboncito to the council:

his brother, Delgadito; his friends Manuelito and Herrero; the statesmanlike Armijo; and two other headmen, Largo and Torivo.

General Sherman opened the negotiations as though the Navajo elders were on trial: "We wish to hear from you the truth and nothing but the truth," he said. "Before we discuss what we are to do with you we want to know what you have done in the past and what you think about your reservation here."

Barboncito answered for the group: "Bringing us here has caused a great decrease of our numbers. Many of us have died, as well as a great number of our animals. Our forefathers had no idea that we should live in any other country except our own. I do not think it right for us to do so. We were never taught to."

The Indian explained, in some detail, about the four sacred mountains marking the boundaries of Dinetah and how it was preordained that The People should live there and in no other place.

"I think that our coming here has been the cause of so much death among us," he said. "The ground we were brought to is not productive. We plant but it does not yield. The stock we brought here have nearly all died.

"We have done all that we could possibly do but have found it to be labor in vain. This ground was never intended for us. We know how to irrigate and how to farm, still we cannot raise a crop here. Outside our own country we cannot raise a crop; in it we can raise crops almost anywhere. There our families and stock increase; here they decrease. We know that this land does not like us.

"It seems that whatever we do here causes death. Some work at the acequias [irrigation ditches] and take sick and die. Others die with the hoe in their hands. A rattlesnake bite here kills us; in our own country a rattlesnake before he bites give warning. In the winter many die from cold and sickness and overwork in carrying wood such a long distance on their backs.

"We have all declared that we do not want to remain here any longer. As you see yourselves, I am strong and hearty. Before I am sick or old I want to go back to the place where I was born. If we are taken back to our own country we will regard you as our father and mother.

"All that you have heard is the truth, and is the opinion of the whole tribe. I am speaking to you now as if I was speaking to a Spirit [that is, in absolute truthfulness], and I wish you to tell me when you are going to take us to our own country."

General Sherman unfolded a map and spread it on the table. "We have got a map here which, if Barboncito can understand, I would like to show him a few points on it," he said.

"For many years we have been collecting Indians on the Indian Territory south of the Arkansas [Oklahoma territory] and they are now doing well and have been doing so for many years. We have heard you were not satisfied with this reservation and we have come here to invite some of your leading men to go and see this country and if they liked it we would give you a reservation there.

"If you do not want that, we will discuss the other proposition of going back to your own country, and if we agree we will make a boundary line outside of which you must not go except for the purpose of trading."

To Barboncito and the others, an inspection tour of Indian Territory would be a waste of time. Sherman pressed the matter, pointing out that the trip would be "at government expense." The Navajo headmen were unimpressed.

"I hope to God," Barboncito replied, "you will not ask me to go to any other country except my own. It might turn out to be another Bosque Redondo. They told us this was a good place when we came, but it is not."

"We merely made the proposition for you to think seriously over it," Sherman said. "Tomorrow at 10 o'clock I want the whole tribe to assemble at the back of the hospital and for you then to delegate ten of your men to come forward and settle about the boundary line of your own country which will be reduced to writing and signed by those ten men."

"We do not want to go to the right or left," Barboncito insisted, "but straight back to our own country."

That night General Sherman argued the alternatives with his fellow commissioner, Senator Tappan. Sherman strongly favored sending the tribe to Indian Territory. Tappan saw no advantage in it. He pointed out that the Navajos' own country, on closer inspection, was worthless. Why not let them have it, or at least a portion of it? Sherman yielded. Writing later about the treaty discussions he said, "After debating all the country at our option we have chosen a small part of their old country which is as far out of the way of the whites and of our future probable wants as possible."

So it was decided, The People would return to Dinetah. Had General Sherman's view prevailed and the Navajos been forever banished from the only spot on the earth where they could find nourishment for their souls, there is little doubt that their culture, like that of the transplanted

Cherokees, would have withered on the parched plains of Oklahoma Territory.

The next morning, General Sherman addressed The People. He told them of his offer to send them to Indian Territory and of Barboncito's refusal. He asked if they had selected ten men to represent them. They had: Barboncito, Manuelito, Delgadito, Herrero, Armijo, and five others—Largo, Chiqueto, Muerto de Hombre, Hombre, and a headman called Narbona, namesake of the old sachem who first discussed peace with the Americans. Sherman asked the ten to select a spokesman. They chose Barboncito unanimously.

"From this time on you must do as Barboncito tells you," the general said. "With him we will deal and do all for your good. When you leave here and go to your own country you must do as he tells you.

"All these things will be put down on paper and tomorrow these ten men will sign that paper. We heard Barboncito yesterday. If there are any others who differ with him we would like to hear them." None spoke.

Barboncito outlined for General Sherman the shortest route back—the route he had once taken himself. He would like the tribe to return that way, he said. The general agreed. There was another matter. Among The People were some who lived near Cebolleta, outside the designated reservation, whom The People regarded as Dineanaih, The People Who Are Enemies. Barboncito asked what his responsibilities towards them would be. The implication was clear. He did not want the Dineanaih on the reservation, in the very heart of Dinetah, nor did he want jurisdiction over them elsewhere.

"If they choose," said Sherman, "they can go and live

among the [New] Mexicans in the Territory. But if they do, they will not be entitled to any advantages of the treaty."

"I merely wished to mention it," Barboncito said. "If they remain with the Mexicans I will not be held responsible for their conduct."

Barboncito had one final point to settle. "I want to talk about Navajo children held as prisoners by Mexicans. Some of those present [that is, the ten] have lost a brother or a sister and I know that they are in the hands of Mexicans. I have seen some myself."

"We do not know that there are any Navajos held by Mexicans as peons," Sherman replied. "If there are, you can apply to the judges of the civil courts and the land commissioners. They are the proper persons, and they will decide whether the Navajo is to go back to his own people or to remain with the Mexicans."

"How many Navajos are among the Mexicans now?" Senator Tappan asked.

"Over half the tribe."

General Sherman was startled at the claim. "We will do all we can to have your children returned to you," he said. "Our government is determined that the enslavement of the Navajos shall cease and those who are guilty of holding them as peons shall be punished."

The council adjourned to the next day. All that night the ten headmen discussed the proceedings with their followers. General Sherman and Senator Tappan, with their clerks, busied themselves drawing up the treaty.

The next morning Sherman read the treaty to Barboncito and the other nine. They nodded their agreement as the terms were tediously translated from English to Spanish and from Spanish to Navajo. When the general finished, Barboncito asked if two other headmen, Narbona Segundo and Ganado Mucho, could be admitted to the tribal council. Already the appointed Navajo chief was troubled about speaking for those whom, according to The People's customs, he did not represent. It is doubtful that General Sherman understood Barboncito's concern, but he did allow the two additional councilmen.

Sherman then told the anxious group that since the next day was Sunday the formal signing would have to wait for two days. The Navajos, whose own religious beliefs were regarded as puerile superstition by their white counterparts, nevertheless did not challenge the reason for the delay.

On Monday morning, June 1, 1868, in a brief ceremony on the Fort Sumner parade ground, the twelve tribal leaders stepped forward to make their Xs at the bottom of a 2,500-word document. It was the first treaty ever made with them in the presence of at least half the tribe; Barboncito asked that six other headmen be allowed to sign it as well, which they did.

For their part, the Navajos promised never again to make war on Americans, Mexicans, or other Indians. For its part, the United States agreed to set aside 5,500 square miles of the Navajos' former homeland for their reservation; allotted the tribe 14,000 sheep and 1,000 goats collectively, an average of two animals per person; pledged many thousands of dollars' worth of farming implements and other items of rehabilitation; promised a clothing allowance of five dollars a year for ten years for every Navajo—ten dollars a year if the recipient could prove he had been industrious and had planted crops; and, finally, the United States of America solemnly promised to provide the Navajos with a school for every thirty children that the Navajos could induce to attend.

The soldiers required more than two weeks to get themselves ready for the trip back; The People were ready from the day of the signing.

Finally, at dawn on June 18, The People left Hwelte. A government clerk, with meticulous care, made the final count: "7,111 Navajo Indians, *viz*: 2,157 under 12 years of age, 2,693 women, 2,060 men, and 201 age and sex unknown."

Smiling through their hunger-drawn faces, joyous despite their pain, they began their long walk home, exiles no longer. Day after day they walked, a procession of quickening pulses stretching ten miles across the land. After three weeks the misty peak of Mount Taylor rose above the horizon and beckoned them to hurry. Three weeks later The People touched their sacred soil, Dinetah.

UP FROM EXILE

EAGLES UNCHAINED, BADGERS UNCAGED

CHAPTER FIFTEEN

"When dealing with savage men, as with savage beasts, no question of national honor can arise. Whether to fight, to run away, or to employ a ruse, is solely a question of expediency," declared United States Commissioner of Indian Affairs Francis C. Walker in 1871. The Navajos had been well aware of their government's official cynicism ever since the day they walked home three years before.

In a memorandum to Senator Tappan two months after The People's repatriation, Agent John Ward sadly reported from Fort Defiance, "Most of the stipulations entered into with the tribe have in most cases been violated on our part. Of the many promises which from time to time have been made to them, scarcely any have ever been properly fulfilled."

134

Even Agent Ward, sympathetic though he seemed, had doubts about one promise—the one General Sherman had made to Barboncito to "do all we can to have your children returned to you." To free Navajo slaves might be a tactical mistake, the agent told the senator, because the captives had been privy to much vital information during their captivity in New Mexican homes. "The knowledge of many of these captives respecting the settlements, the people and their mode of living, the localities where their herds and flocks are usually kept," wrote Ward, "all of this would be of great advantage to the Navajos in the event of another open war and even in making simple raids. All of which ought to be duly considered."

Because only expediency and not national honor was involved, as the commissioner in Washington observed, other promises were similarly flouted. It was fifteen months before the government delivered the sheep and horses it had pledged to the Navajos. It was fifteen *years* before other treaty goods trickled out to New Mexico. The Navajo agent calculated that by 1886 the government had ignored its treaty promises to the extent of $792,000.

The People were further saddened in early 1871 when their beloved Barboncito died, broken in spirit and dejected by his inability to help his people as he wished. His close friends dressed him in new clothes and jewelry and put his moccasins on the wrong feet so that his spirit would not make tracks like a living man. Then they covered their own bodies with ashes from a ceremonial plant to ward off the evil spirits, carried the dead man's body through a hole broken in the north side of his hogan, and set fire to the hogan. Next to him at the place of burial they left his saddle and bridle. They took his horse to another place and killed it with its head pointing to the east. For four days The People mourned Barboncito, and after that they did not speak his name again.

No one headman could command the widespread respect of Barboncito. Designated to replace him, as co-chiefs, were two men of great stature among The People, Manuelito and Ganado Mucho, both of whom had signed the treaty of 1868.

Although the Navajos suffered and starved on their return to Dinetah, their psychological relief was more than adequate compensation. They were destitute, but they were home; the eagles were unchained, the badgers uncaged. They held Enemy Way ceremonies to purge the alien contagions of their exile, sought out the scattered groups of their brethren who had escaped Kit Carson's noose (The People called Carson "The Rope Thrower"), and dispersed throughout their paradise regained to pick up the threads of horribly ruptured lives.

New energy came to them in their Promised Land, a godsend in the truest sense. Restored to the bosom of Changing Woman, their devastated fields flowered again, and on the hillsides flocks grazed. Left alone, The People's comeback was incredibly swift. In ten years they built their sheep flock from 14,000 animals to 700,000—a fifty-fold increase. "They have grown from a band of paupers to a nation of prosperous, industrious, shrewd and (for barbarians) intelligent people," marveled the agent at Fort Defiance in a report. One can assume that the agent added the parenthetical slur either because he believed it or because he simply wanted to reassure Washington that he was faithfully adhering to official thinking.

The People's population doubled in thirty years, and as

their numbers increased (along with the size of their herds and flocks), they predictably spilled over their unrealistic reservation boundaries. The surrounding lands, over which so much blood had been spent in the course of a generation, had remained unsettled by whites during the Navajos' exile and during the years after their return. Once he had driven the despised barbarians off the land, the white man's lust for it quickly cooled. The grass on the other side of the fence proved to be no greener after all.

Had the Navajos been aware of American homestead laws they could have regained title to all their former land simply by building the required "improvements," but a hogan did not fit the white definition of a home. In any case, the Interior Department recognized the obvious: the Indians were living outside their reservation, and no whites objected. The solution was equally obvious: to give the Indians the land. By the simple expedient of an executive order, President Rutherford B. Hayes did just that in 1878.

It was the beginning of a process that made all the anguish and suffering that had gone before, from Doniphan's expedition to The Long Walk, one of history's most bitter ironies. Each time the Navajos overflowed onto adjoining, uninhabited land, a presidential executive order made that land a part of their reservation. It happened fourteen times. Finally, the Navajo reservation came to include 25,000 square miles, its present area—not all the land embraced by the four sacred mountains, to be sure, but far more than the 7,000 square miles set aside by David Meriwether in 1855 as the limits of the first Navajo reservation.

Indian Commissioner Walker, of course, had confidently expected the Navajos to fade away once they were dumped back onto the "small part of their own country which is as far out of the way of the whites and of our future probable wants as possible." This time the ruse backfired.

Towards the end of the nineteenth century, when the last of the Plains tribes had been thoroughly beaten and humiliated—"tamed" was the usual verb—Indians came to be regarded more or less as national household pets. Dime novelists and wild west show entrepreneurs found profit in romanticizing the "noble red man," but most Americans regarded him as a cigar-store ornament.

The Navajos were no exception. "They are a most interesting race of barbarians," wrote one visitor to Fort Defiance, J. H. Beadle, who went on to observe that "like most savage races, their religion is principally superstition." Another scholar, Jonathan Letterman, spent three years on the reservation and reported his discoveries to the Smithsonian Institution. "Of their religion," he wrote of The People, "little or nothing is known, as, indeed, all inquiries tend to show that they have none. . . . The lack of tradition is a source of surprise. They have no knowledge of their origin or of the history of the tribe."

The unsophisticated Henry Linn Dodge lived among The People with an open mind and found them to be neither quaint nor barbaric but richly endowed human beings. He was not typical; the learned Letterman and Beadle were. They reflected the prevailing, centuries-old American position regarding the Indian, a position of racial superiority, cultural arrogance, and blind ignorance.

Thus The People were not surprised at what they found when, in 1881, a wagonload of supplies arrived at Fort

Defiance in accordance with the treaty. Unloading the governmental largess, the Navajos discovered such items as suspenders, high-button shoes, and sixty-four dozen sets of furniture casters. At least the barrels that they came in were useful.

As in the old days, it was all but impossible for the Navajos to keep track of who was who in the American government. In thirty years, the agency at Fort Defiance changed hands fifteen times, and there were long periods when there was no agent at all.

In one respect the Navajos benefited from the high turnover. Some of the bewildering assortment of regulations emanating from Washington mercifully failed to reach them, such as the decree of 1884 forbidding Indian religious practices. (That law stood until 1933 and was invoked as late as 1926 to cast into jail the Taos Pueblo's entire governing body for keeping boys out of school to observe puberty rites.) Another such decree was the Dawes Act of 1887, more commonly called the General Allotment Act; it assigned quarter-section plots to individual Indians so that landless whites could have the "surplus" of their reservation. This was done "on behalf of the Indians," relieving them of some ninety million acres. Sen. Henry L. Dawes of Massachusetts saw the need of it when he visited Indian Territory. "The defect of the reservation system," he said, "was apparent. They have got as far as they can go, because they own their land in common. . . . There is no selfishness, which is at the bottom of civilization." Said President Grover Cleveland, Pilate-like, as he signed the Dawes Act: "The hunger and thirst of the white man for the Indian's land is almost equal to his hunger and thirst after righteousness."

Some laws did, however, find their way to Navajoland. Two such laws were the law of 1886 which said that no Indian child could be sent to a reservation school without his parents' consent and the law of 1887 which made school attendance compulsory.

The latter law loosed a wave of terror throughout Dinetah almost as traumatic as Kit Carson's roundup. Eager deputies scoured the countryside, snatched children from fields and hogans—in truth kidnapping them—and hauled them to Fort Defiance. From there they were sent to a boarding school at Fort Lewis, Colorado, where they slept three to a bunk and ate on a budget of seven cents a day per child. They also got their hair cut and were taught to feel inferior. Some escaped, just as their parents had escaped from Hwelte, and some died trying to find their way home. Many parents were never informed about the law and never knew what had become of their children. Eventually, so that the children would not have to be sent so far away, a boarding school was built at Fort Defiance. It had bars on the windows.

To most white Americans of the nineteenth century, a visit to the Navajo reservation to learn about The People meant no more than a trip to Fort Defiance to chat with the agent. Few, including the agent, ventured far into the trackless regions where The People lived, even as today's tourists and college students discover little beyond the radius of a day's motor-trip from the nearest air-conditioned motel; they visit the reservation as they would a zoo, to view exhibits that have come out of the wilds.

This was decidedly untrue of one specific group of whites, however, and their impact on The People's lives was greater than that of any bureaucrat, schoolmarm, anthropologist, or missionary. These were the Indian traders who lived among the Navajos.

Not the motion picture villain who sold watered whisky and faulty guns from the back of a wagon and then moved on, but men like Henry Linn Dodge, who cast their lots with the Navajos through good times and bad. Over the years some scoundrels did turn up in their ranks. One earned the Navajo name Man Who Steps on Us. He and his kind were, and are, the exceptions. As a group, the traders to the Navajos were the only white Americans who came neither to exterminate their red brothers, "civilize" them, proselyte them, nor to exploit them. They came to barter, not to judge.

The first trader came to the Navajo reservation in 1875. Fifteen years later there were eight more traders on the reservation and about thirty in the area surrounding it. The Navajos brought their wool and rugs to the traders and swapped them for beans and sugar; they brought their silver bracelets and pawned them for saddles; and they brought their troubles, to receive understanding and help. The trading posts were far more than supply depots. They were centers for news and gossip and meeting places for families who came from surrounding areas of hundreds of square miles and stayed for days. Some of the visitors slept at night on the trader's floor; the door was not locked.

To the traders the Navajos owe the nationwide popularity of their exquisite blankets, rugs, and jewelry. The People's life was often reduced to bare essentials, and one of those essentials was their art. If J. H. Beadle was no expert on religion as practiced by "barbarians," he at least knew good weaving when he saw it. Here is his report:

Their blankets are the wonder of all who see them. They are woven by the squaws in a rude frame, and are so compact that water can be carried in them four or five hours before it begins to leak through. . . . The woolen yarn for "filling" is made from their own sheep, generally, and is of three colors, black, white and red from native coloring. Running these together by turns with nimble fingers the squaw brings out on the blanket squares, diamonds, circles and fanciful curves, and flowers of three colors, with a skill which is simply amazing. Two months are required to complete an ordinary blanket, five feet wide and eight long. . . . One will outlast a lifetime; and though rolled in the mud, or daubed with grease for months or years, until every vestige of color seems gone, when washed with the soap weed [yucca roots], the bright native colors come out as beautiful as ever.

Aside from the fact that the Navajos did not use the Iroquoian word "squaw" for their women and that their weavers were by no means restricted to such a limited range of colors, Mr. Beadle's description was quite accurate. So was his afterthought, a comment on the "unwearying patience they display in all of their work and their zeal and quickness to learn in everything which may improve their condition. Surely such a people are capable of civilization." Like many other white Americans, Mr. Beadle confused civilization with industrialization.

When the railroad reached the Southwest the Navajo traders saw to it that The People's blankets and artifacts spread across the land, from the parlors of Park Avenue to the drawing rooms of Nob Hill.

But the trading posts were more than export centers. The trader was the one constant and reliable link between the white world and the Navajo. Very nearly every white person who came to the reservation soon left, except the trader. The trader came to know The People, and they him. He learned their language and their beliefs. He doctored their sheep. He buried their dead. He interpreted for them the latest government decrees, and he could be trusted.

Through the trader, The People gradually learned about the country that had overwhelmed them, its government, and its people. Fortified with that knowledge, they began to venture more and more into the cities that were rapidly growing up around the reservation. Indians on city streets were reviled, threatened, abused, humiliated, and made to stand aside, but not all the time and not by everyone. Little by little The People gained confidence in their contacts with the alien culture drawing ever tighter around them.

Americans observed the turn of the century only thirty-two years after the Navajos' return from Fort Sumner. No non-Navajo can fully appreciate the wrenching effect of The Long Walk and the total disruption of the equilibrium of Navajo life. Stories of personal experiences during that dreadful epoch have been handed down and carefully preserved in family traditions. Mention of The Long Walk even finds its way into ceremonials.

Yet when the United States entered World War I a good number of Navajos volunteered to serve in the American army, sons of parents who survived that very army's concentration camp on the Bosque Redondo. Other Indians also volunteered, likewise sons of fathers whose blood had stained U.S. Cavalry sabers.

In return for that service the United States Government

in 1924 granted American citizenship to the Indian, the only true native of the soil.

That did not mean he could vote. Just as racist lawmakers in the South refused to allow the Negro to vote unless his grandfather, who was a slave, had voted, clever officials contrived ways to deny the Indian his fundamental right of citizenship. Arizona refused Navajos the vote because they were "persons under guardianship"; New Mexico, because they did not pay taxes. Both of those transparent legalisms lasted for another generation.

THE PEOPLE TODAY

A NEW FLOWERING OF CULTURAL PRIDE

CHAPTER SIXTEEN

Most Americans remember the favorite childhood pastime of "cowboys and Indians." The author recalls one Saturday afternoon most vividly. While bravely defending the wagon train, I peeked over my shield (a garbage-can lid) and very nearly got my eye put out by a well-aimed arrow. Usually, however, the whooping and cavorting of the mock battles were never as loud or as serious as the arguments over who would be the cowboys and who the Indians. Nobody wanted to start out as a loser.

A cherished role those Saturday afternoons was that of the Indian scout, the good Indian. He was an enigmatic creature who had wisely and humbly forsaken the path of war for the path of righteousness. But he retained his animal-like stealth and cunning and spoke in grunts, qualities greatly admired by boys. He felt honored to be allowed to saddle the cavalry officer's horse and walk two paces behind. He too could be on the winning side, provided that he allowed a compassionate, white leader to supply the brains. This was the good Indian of an American boy's literature in the 1930s. Nothing he heard in school taught him differently.

For an American boy's parents, however, the thirties were a time of fewer certainties. The nation's economy was a shambles. Americans were willing to question old formulas and challenge old assumptions and to ask themselves what they were and what they could be as Americans. They wanted a New Deal.

John Collier, the man President Franklin D. Roosevelt appointed as Indian commissioner, was determined that the first Americans would share in that New Deal. He drew up an Indian Reorganization Bill which, among other provisions, would allow Indians to have a voice in their own recovery from a reservation life of poverty and neglect. John Collier was the most farsighted Indian commissioner to hold the office up to that time, as well as the most scholarly and dedicated. (It remained for a future president, Lyndon B. Johnson, to establish the principle that the Indian commissioner should be an Indian.)

Commissioner Collier took his Reorganization Bill to the reservations and asked the tribes to vote on it before he submitted it to Congress. The Navajos turned it down. The white man's long history of treachery and broken promises made The People wary of any deal, old or new, with the federal government. Enough other tribes favored the bill, however, that Congress passed the act in 1934. The Navajos eventually shared in its benefits.

Its most far-reaching provision was for tribal self-government. The venerable Navajo elders—Barboncito, Manuelito, Ganado Mucho, and their successors, "chiefs" appointed by the agent at Fort Defiance—were in no real sense heads of government. Nor was the tribal council organized for the Navajos in 1923 a true governing body. It met for two days a year in the presence of a government official and was so meaningless that the few tribesmen who knew the council existed generally ignored it. In 1938, however, a Navajo Tribal Government was formed which grew steadily in strength and effectiveness among the tribe. It consisted of an elected chairman and vice-chairman, and seventy-four delegates representing nineteen reservation districts. The concept of elected spokesmen remained strange to the Navajos, and over the years many have had difficulty accepting council decisions in which they did not participate. But the overall experience resulted in an increasing alertness among The People to the ways of America and Americans.

The Navajos needed to be ever alert. Like General Carleton, Agent Graves, and other predators dating back to the Conquistadores, some persons in governmental authority seemed never able to rid themselves of the notion that there was gold in the Navajos' hills—white man's gold. In 1891 the Interior Department—charged, it should be remembered, with the responsibility of protecting the interests of the Indians—appointed a three-man commission "to negotiate with the Navajo Indians in Arizona and New Mexico for the surrender of a portion of their reservation." (To "negotiate" a "surrender" didn't seem contradictory among those dealing with Indians.) Happily for the Navajos the acting commissioner of Indian affairs, after a year-long survey of the reservation, was forced to send this sad report to the secretary of interior: "The commissioners state that in view of the disappointing fact that no bodies of ore-carrying values have been found in the Carrizo Mountains they did not deem it any part of their duty to proceed with negotiation. . . ."

In 1921 official thievery came even closer. Not a precious metal but a precious mineral—oil—was discovered on the Navajo reservation. Immediately, Secretary of the Interior Albert Fall tried to get his hands on it. He issued an order which said that the oil rightly belonged to the federal government, not the Indians. The reason, he explained with wide-eyed innocence, was that the oil was on land added to the Navajo reservation by presidential executive order, as opposed to the original 1868 treaty land. The Navajos objected, of course, and Congress reversed the Fall order five years later. In 1931, Albert Fall was in jail in connection with the Elk Hills and Teapot Dome scandals. As the years passed, The People were kept busy combatting attempts to bilk them out of their land and resources.

John Collier may well have saved the Navajos from extinction. He did so through a program that many of The People never understood. Many in fact despised him for his program—livestock reduction.

Since their return from Fort Sumner, The People had built their sheep flocks to an incredible total of 1,370,000 animals by 1931. The range could not support them. On parts of the reservation, grass was so sparse that a single sheep had to scour fifty acres to get enough food. The animals grew scrawny. The land was so badly eroded that 45 percent of its topsoil had been washed away. There was only one solution. The People had to be told to get rid of most of their sheep. The Navajo Tribal Council concurred.

Sheep, as The People say, represent "that which men live by." They allow no part of that precious animal to go to waste. After they roast the juicy ribs they stuff the stomach with a blood-and-fat dressing and boil it. The heart and lungs are fried and the intestines roasted. The head and feet are cooked in ashes. The bones make soup and the pelt a rug.

For decades the government had exhorted The People to build up their flocks. Now the order was to reduce them. One can understand the Navajos' consternation.

The livestock-reduction program brought on another era of trauma and confusion for The People. The recollection of one Navajo, Dan Phillips, is typical: "Although we were told that it was to restore the land, the fact remains that hunger and poverty stood with their mouths open to devour us. Before the stock that remained could reproduce, people slit the animals' throats to satisfy their starving children." But the program worked. By 1943 livestock had been reduced by nearly two-thirds. The grass grew taller, the sheep fatter, and their fleece thicker.

At the same time, another climactic episode, World War II, engulfed The People and propelled them into what could be considered their modern era. When the war broke out, Blessing Way ceremonies were held with great frequency across the reservation as thirty-six hundred young Navajo men went off to fight. Most of them carried buckskin pouches of corn pollen as their comrades carried religious medals. Navajo soldiers distinguished themselves. Especially acclaimed was a unit of twenty-nine marine "code talkers" whose Navajo language utterly baffled the Japanese. Today one of those code talkers is a tribal judge and another heads the tribe's economic-opportunity program.

Three years after the war, the courts struck down the flimsy legal charades that had prevented Navajos from voting. And after Indian soldiers returned home from a third war, in Korea, a grateful government decided (in 1953) that it would no longer be illegal for an Indian to buy liquor.

The reservation that the Navajos returned to after those wars was a pitiful caricature of America's celebrated prosperity. To cite one measure of living standards, the Navajo diet was only twelve hundred calories a day. That was about one-third the nutritional level of their former comrades-in-arms and considerably less than that enjoyed by their former foes, the war-ravaged Japanese and Germans. As another measure of reservation conditions, one of every two Navajo children died before the age of five.

Too many returning Navajo veterans had had a glimpse of another life to be content with their lot. They saw that they could no longer hide from the federal government's influence as they had once hidden from Kit Carson's troops, nor could they deal with the government strictly as antagonist. Each day more Navajos realized that they needed federal assistance, that it was owed to them, and that if they were cautious and intelligent they could enjoy its benefits without allowing it to corrupt their culture.

Education, despite the long history of terror and cruelty at government schools, was seen as a twentieth-century necessity. Age-old obstacles remained and had to be changed. "We were rarely taught enough of what we needed to know to survive in a highly technological society," said a Navajo who endured those early, postwar years, "but we were always taught how bad, mean and vicious we Indians were."

The People swallowed hard and saw it through. They dragged out the old treaty and reminded the federal government of its 1868 agreement to provide a school and teacher for every thirty Navajo children. Nothing even approaching that standard has been reached, but today there are forty-six government schools on or near the reservation, and nearly all forty thousand reservation children attend them. School enrollment more than tripled from 1950 to 1970. The number of high-school graduates jumped from seventy-five to fifteen hundred a year. Not satisfied with that, the tribe set aside $10 million of its oil revenue as a college scholarship trust fund. In 1970 about six hundred Navajos were in college and the tribal chairman was a college graduate—the first in Navajo history. In 1969, a year after The People observed the centennial of their liberation from the Bosque Redondo, the Navajo Community College opened on the reservation at Many Farms, Arizona, the first institution of higher learning to be operated by an Indian tribe. The Navajos also organized their own education association, called *Dineh Biolta*, The People's Schools. The tribe hopes eventually to take over the government schools completely, run them themselves, and staff them with Navajo-thinking, Navajo-speaking Navajos. So determined are they to cling to their culture that in 1970 they began a program in which parents visit boarding schools and discuss Navajo lore with the students. Even in 1970 the job of education was extremely difficult because 80 percent of the reservation children starting school spoke little or no English; their teachers, by and large, were Anglos who spoke no Navajo.

"The Navajo people are no longer content to let the white man run their schools," said Ned Hatathli, president of the Navajo Community College. "By 1980 we do not think there will be a single school on the reservation not controlled by the Navajo people. We do not know the form it will take. During the 1970s the principle of Navajo control over Navajo schools will be practiced as well as preached. We will have, for the first time, the right to be wrong, if that is the case."

The People's concept of illness and its causes is such that only one Navajo has thus far been able to make the psychological adjustments necessary to pursue a medical career. That man, Dr. Taylor McKenzie, completed medical school and returned to the reservation to serve his people as chief surgeon at one of the reservation hospitals. Dr. McKenzie believes that, as with Navajo schools, Navajo hospitals ought to be run by Navajos. "There are certain decisions about medical and health services relating to and affecting Navajos which only Navajos can make," Dr. McKenzie said. "These decisions, if made unilaterally by the hospital and its [white] staff, would only engender resentment and suspicion. These difficult decisions would more readily be acceptable to The People if they were made by a local board of Navajos."

The tribe put its mineral resources to work in ways other than providing college scholarships. Oil, gas, and uranium royalties and bonuses reached a peak of $33 million in 1956 but now bring in about a third of that a year.

Rather than spread it thinly among individual families, the tribal council decided to make the money work for all The People. It goes for water wells, health benefits, housing programs, roads, various tribal services, and further development of the reservation's natural resources.

The tribe built a $7.5 million sawmill which turns out 50 million board-feet of lumber a year and employs 450 men. In conjunction with the federal government The People have embarked on an irrigation project which, beginning in 1971, will pipe enough water to cultivate 111,000 acres of what is now arid desert. At the site of old Fort Defiance, long a symbol of oppression to The People, a cluster of busy industries stands as a symbol of their ambition—Fort Defiance Industrial Park.

The tribe established its capital at a spot sacred to them about six miles from the old fort site. Window Rock, Arizona, a place known to The People as *Tseghanhodzani*, is one of four places where singers can go to collect water in woven bottles for *Tohee*, the Water Way ceremony, held to assure abundant rain. There, today, the seventy-four-member Navajo Tribal Council meets in a chamber constructed in the fashion of a large hogan, with murals by Navajo artists adorning the walls. A far cry from the ineffective council of twelve that Barboncito presided over in 1868, today's tribal council makes decisions affecting tens of thousands of tribesmen and administers an annual budget of some $15 million. One of the most respected members of that council, incidentally, is a man who has served on it for more than twenty-five years, Howard Gorman, a grandson of the revered Barboncito and a *bizahalani*, a "man of eloquence," in his own right. Other descendants of those Navajo heroes who felt Kit

Carson's lash have likewise served on the modern-day council. Council discussions and debates are conducted in Navajo and patiently translated into English for the benefit of visitors and government officials.

Near the council chamber are buildings housing a tribal newspaper, health and welfare offices, a credit union, and the offices of *Dinebeiina Nahiilna Be Agaditahe*, the Navajo legal-aid service. In one of the tribal offices a computer, the supreme symbol of the American corporation, hums away keeping track of tribal enterprises; nearby stands a modern motel, the Window Rock Inn, owned by the tribe.

Any impression that the Navajos are wallowing in oil riches, however, ought to be quickly put aside. The People have a long way to go to catch up with the standard of living surrounding their reservation. The average family income on the reservation is still only about one thousand dollars a year. The Navajo infant mortality rate is still twice that of the general population of the country. A survey conducted from 1963 to 1967 at one of the reservation's six hospitals disclosed that nearly 15 percent of the children admitted suffered from malnutrition. Among them were forty-four cases of *kwashiorkor*, a nutritional disease almost unheard of in the United States. Such is life on the Navajo reservation.

Why, then, do The People stay? Why do they not leave and blend into American society? One Navajo who came back from college to live and work on the reservation explained, "There is a little candle burning inside every Navajo that makes him realize he is a Navajo, a little candle that never goes out." The changes that the twentieth century has brought to the Navajo have been outward, not inward. Inwardly, the Navajo barreling down Highway 66 in his pickup truck on his way to Arizona State College is little different from the Navajo who hid his children from the boarding-school kidnappers.

No Navajo would deny that he wants desperately to escape from poverty and enjoy as many material benefits as other Americans do, but not at any price. He is not at all convinced of white America's moral and cultural superiority. During the civil-rights struggles of the 1960s the Navajos remained aloof. Integration was not for them. They prefer their own culture. "In view of the white man's inability to create a world in which all can live together in peace," said an editorial in the *Navajo Times*, "the Indian's religion and culture have grown in stature."

Navajos today are growing more conscious of their unique culture and more appreciative of it. A new awareness of their own identity and a new tribal pride is banishing any feelings of inferiority that may still linger.

The history of the Navajos is that of a people who for centuries lived together without jails, orphanages, asylums, or welfare agencies. Their culture provided its own solutions to social problems quite satisfactorily. The more The People learn of white culture, the more convinced they become of the worth of their own. When the tribe observed the 100th anniversary of the Treaty of 1868, their centennial proclamation declared: "We are fortunate that we have been returned some of our beloved land secure within the four sacred mountains guarding us and our ways." Their ways, not the ways of the predominant culture. To paraphrase Navajo Chief Justice Murray Lincoln, the white man surely has as much to learn from The People as he has to teach them.

A new flowering of cultural pride is not the only reason for the fondness every Navajo feels for the reservation. There is something far more compelling than that which lures back to the reservation every third Navajo who leaves it. On the reservation, and only on the reservation, time stands still for a Navajo, and the world becomes whole. There, and only there, all of life pulses with the sweet, magic rhythms that have sustained The People for all of time and have taught them the trick of quiet. There, mystery whispers in the yucca blossoms and plays overhead in the aspen boughs. There, and only there, is Dinetah, the land of The People.

There a Navajo can stand at the yawning mouth of Blue Canyon and listen in wonder to the eerie screams of Naked Woman on Horseback, who dwells within. There he can raise his eyes to Bennett Peak by night and dare to glimpse the saffron glow of witches' fires. There he can see the cottonwood turn golden in the fall and see the wildflower bloom and the peach ripen and rejoice that Changing Woman is close at hand. There he can listen to the soft call of the mourning dove, the little brother of the Navajo who also wears red moccasins, and know that rain is in the air. There, and only there, a Navajo can walk daily in the favor and in the footsteps of his gods.

With beauty before me I walk.
With beauty behind me I walk.
With beauty below me I walk.
With beauty above me I walk.
With beauty all around me I walk.
I will be happy forever,
Nothing will hinder me. . . .

FOR FURTHER READING

Bailey, Lynn R. *The Long Walk: A History of the Navajo Wars, 1846–68.* Los Angeles: Western Lore, 1964.

Blumenthal, Walter Hart. *American Indians Dispossessed.* Philadelphia: George S. MacManus Co., 1955.

Collier, John. *Indians of the Americas.* New York: New American Library, Mentor Books, 1961.

Dyk, Walter. *Son of Old Man Hat.* Lincoln: University of Nebraska Press, 1938.

Farb, Peter. *Man's Rise to Civilization as Shown by the Indians of North America from Primeval Times to the Coming of the Industrial State.* New York: E. P. Dutton & Co., 1968.

Ferguson, Erna. *New Mexico.* New York: Alfred A. Knopf, 1951.

Gillmor, Frances, and Wetherill, Louisa Wade. *Traders to the Navajos: The Story of the Wetherills of Kayenta.* Albuquerque: The University of New Mexico Press, 1953.

Kluckhohn, Clyde, and Leighton, Dorothea. *The Navaho.* Cambridge: Harvard University Press, 1946.

Lipps, Oscar H. *The Navajos.* Cedar Rapids: Torch Press, 1909.

McCall, George Archibald. *New Mexico in 1850: A Military View.* Norman: University of Oklahoma Press, 1968.

Moorhead, Max L. *The Apache Frontier.* Norman: University of Oklahoma Press, 1968.

Sabin, Edwin L. *Kit Carson Days, 1809–1869: Adventures in the Path of Empire.* New York: Press of the Pioneers, 1935.

Spencer, Robert F., and Jennings, Jesse D. *The Native Americans.* New York: Harper & Row, 1965.

Underhill, Ruth M. *The Navajos.* Norman: University of Oklahoma Press, 1956.

Washburn, Wilcomb E., ed. *The Indian and the White Man.* New York: Doubleday & Co., Anchor Books, 1964.

Waters, Frank. *Masked Gods: Navajo and Pueblo Ceremonialism.* New York: Ballantine Books, 1950.

Young, Robert W., ed. *The Navajo Yearbook.* Window Rock, Arizona: Bureau of Indian Affairs, The Navajo Agency, 1961.

INDEX

McKenzie, Dr. Taylor, 152
Magellan, Ferdinand, 21
Manifest Destiny, 38
Manuelito (Indian), 92, 93, 94, 105, 126, 127, 130, 136, 147
Marshall, John, 115
Massachusetts Bay Colony, 34, 35
Massasoit, Chief, 34
Mather, Cotton, 34, 91
Mayflower (ship), 34
Meriwether, David, 90, 91, 137
Mescalero Apache tribe, 24, 98, 99, 100, 107
Mexican War, 39–40, 84
Mexico, independence of (1821), 32, 41
Miles, Lieutenant Colonel Dixon S., 93, 94
Missouri Mounted Volunteers, 72
Montezuma, Emperor, 19, 22
Moore, Colonel James, 35
Mount Taylor, 49, 133
Muerto de Hombre (Indian), 130
Museum of Navajo Ceremonial Art, 7
Mythology, 9–10, 13, 33, 55–61
    good and evil, 68–69
    Hero Twins, 64, 66, 110
    legend of origin, 9–10, 16, 67–68
    Spider Woman, 29
    Where We Emerged, 44–51, 67–68, 69

Narbona (Indian), 75, 76, 77, 79, 80, 81, 96
Narbona Segundo, 130, 132
Navajo Community College, 151, 152
Navajo Indians
    arts, 28–29

birth rate, 2
cultural assimilation and, 12–13, 25–26
geographic place names, 55, 57
golden age of, 53
intermarriages, 53
kinship system, 56–58
language, 5–6, 11, 18, 19, 24–25, 55–56
livestock-reduction program, 149
raiding prowess, 26, 44, 53–54, 71, 82–84, 89, 98
religious practices, 8–9, 139
sacredness of name, 11
sense of humor, 7
sense of nationhood, 18
Spanish policy toward, 26–32
suffrage, 150
system of justice, 14
treaties with U.S., 78–81, 91, 94–95, 96, 105, 131–132, 148, 155
uniqueness of, 2
weaving skills, 28–29, 141, 142
See also Reservation (Navajoland)
Navajo Mountain, 55
Navajo Tribal Council, 13, 147, 149, 153–154
Negroes, 20, 93, 144
New Deal, 146
New Mexico, Confederate threat to, 98
New York Morning News, 38
New York Times, The, 37
Newby, Colonel E. W. R 78, 83, 90
Nicknames, 11
Night Way (prayer), 66
Niza, Fray Marcos de, 20